Essential
Caribbean

by Emma Stanford

Emma Stanford has written books
and articles on Florida, California, the
Caribbean, Hawaii, France and Spain,
including *Essential Florida* and *Essential
Orlando* in this series, as well as
Mediterranean ports for the US Navy.
She has also contributed to guides
published by the BTA, American Express,
National Geographic
and Fodor.

Above: *Trunk Bay, St John, US Virgin Islands*

AA Publishing

Written by Emma Stanford

First Published 2000
Reprinted Aug 2000, Jul 2001, Oct 2001, Apr 2002

© 2000 Automobile Association Developments Ltd
Maps © 2000 Automobile Association Developments Ltd

Published by AA Publishing, a trading name of
Automobile Association Developments Limited,
whose registered office is Millstream,
Maidenhead Road, Windsor, Berkshire SL4 5GD.
Registered number 1878835.

The Automobile Association retains the copyright
in the original edition © 2000 and in all subsequent
editions, reprints and amendments.

A CIP catalogue record for this book is available from the
British Library.

ISBN 0 7495 2210 0

Above: *an accordion
player takes his music to
the street in the
Dominican Republic*

The contents of this publication are believed correct at
the time of printing. Nevertheless, the publishers cannot
be held responsible for any errors or omissions or for
changes in the details given in this guide or for the
consequences of any reliance on the information provided
by the same. Assessments of attractions, hotels,
restaurants and so forth are based upon the author's own
experience and, therefore, descriptions given in this guide
necessarily contain an element of subjective opinion which
may not reflect the publisher's opinion or dictate a reader's
own experience on another occasion.

We have tried to ensure accuracy in this guide, but
things do change and we would be grateful if readers
would advise us of any inaccuracies they may encounter.

Colour separation: Chroma Graphics (Overseas) Pte Ltd,
Singapore
Printed and bound in Italy by Printer Trento srl

Find out more about
AA Publishing and the
wide range of services
the AA provides by
visiting our web site at
www.theAA.com

Contents

About this Book

Essential *Caribbean* is divided into five sections to cover the most important aspects of your visit to the Caribbean.

Viewing the Caribbean pages 5–14
An introduction to the Caribbean by the author.
   The Caribbean's Features
   Essence of the Caribbean
   The Shaping of the Caribbean
   Peace and Quiet
   The Caribbean's Famous

Top Ten pages 15–26
The author's choice of the Top Ten places in the Caribbean, listed in alphabetical order, each with practical information.

What to See pages 27–90
The islands have been divided into two sections, East and West, each with its own brief introduction and an alphabetical listing of the main attractions.
   Practical information
   Snippets of 'Did you know…' information
   1 suggested walk
   3 suggested drives
   2 features

Where To... pages 91–116
Detailed listings of the best places to eat, stay, shop, take the children and be entertained.

Practical Matters pages 117–24
A highly visual section containing essential travel information.

Maps
All map references are to the individual maps found in the What to See section of this guide.

For example, Grenada has the reference 🗺 54B2 – indicating the page on which the map is located and the grid square in which the island is to be found. A list of the maps that have been used in this travel guide can be found in the index.

Prices
Where appropriate, an indication of the cost of an establishment is given by £ signs:

£££ denotes higher prices
££ denotes average prices
£ denotes lower charges

Star Ratings
Most of the places described in this book have been given a separate rating:

✪✪✪   Do not miss
✪✪   Highly recommended
✪   Worth seeing

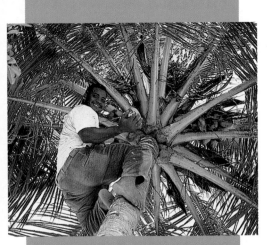

Viewing the
Caribbean

Above: *harvesting coconuts at
Brimmer Hall, Jamaica*
Right: *fresh coconut milk straight from
the shell*

Emma Stanford's Caribbean

Sense and Sensibilities
While Caribbean islanders are friendly and generous hosts, they are also sticklers for a degree of courtesy and modesty. Take time to respond to greetings – a smile and a wave works wonders for international relations. Except on the French islands, topless bathing is not acceptable on beaches frequented by local people, and off the beach women should wear a cotton wrap over swimsuits.

Below: *colourful colonial architecture in Puerto Plata, Dominican Republic*
Bottom: *relaxing on Doctor's Cave beach, Jamaica*

Warm sand between your toes, the rustle of palm trees, bathing in a rainforest waterfall and listening to the chirrup of tree frogs at night are among the small but significant pleasures of a Caribbean holiday. Ever since Christopher Columbus first brought news of their existence to the Spanish court, these delectable, sun-kissed islands have worked their magic on travellers and tourists.

For most visitors a Caribbean holiday is an idyllic escape from the daily grind. Sun, sea and sand are guaranteed in abundance, but look beyond the small but significant comfort of the cruise ship, and the Caribbean's charms are many and varied. Each island has its own special flavour, a combination of geography, history, culture and attitude which can come as a surprise to anyone who ever thought the Caribbean was just...well, the Caribbean.

The legacy of former British islands, such as Antigua and Barbados, includes Georgian architecture, cricket and afternoon tea served with due ceremony in the islands' smartest hotels. Meanwhile, the Spanish Catholic heritage is alive and well in Puerto Rico; Willemstad, the capital of Dutch Curaçao, is a tropical Amsterdam of pastel-painted gabled buildings; and the French Antilles retain the language, culinary traditions and *savoir-faire* of *la belle France*.

Yet, alongside these relics of the Old World, Caribbean culture has developed its own vibrant and colourful identity. Reggae, steel pan, carnivals and craft markets are all intrinsic components of the Caribbean scene. Add to that stunning scenery and the laid-back hospitality of the islanders themselves, and the Caribbean promises all you could ask for, and more.

The Caribbean's Features

Geography

• There are more than 7,000 islands ranged around the Caribbean Sea varying in size from Cuba (42,800 square miles/110,810sq km), the 15th largest island in the world, to tiny coral atolls barely rising above sea-level.

• The most northerly landfall in the Caribbean is on the north coast of Cuba, 90 miles (145km) south of Key West, Florida. Cuba is also the most westerly island; Barbados marks the eastern extent and Trinidad the southern.

• The islands follow a rough arc almost 2,500 miles (4,020km) long, poised above the point where the Caribbean and Atlantic tectonic plates collide.

• Most islands are of volcanic origin with a few low-lying coral outcrops such as the Cayman Islands and Anguilla.

• The Windward Islands, Guadeloupe, Martinique and Montserrat are still volcanically active. The highest volcano is Mont Pelée (4,583ft/1,397m) in Martinique.

• The climate is tropical with average temperatures of 80–83°F (27–29°C) year-round, subject to local variations.

• Average annual rainfall varies from 350in (890cm) in the highlands of Dominica to 10in (25cm) in Bonaire.

Politics

• There are 24 separate political entities in the Caribbean region, including British, French and Dutch colonies, and the US territories of Puerto Rico and the US Virgin Islands.

• The Caribbean Community and Common Market (CARICOM) was founded in 1973 to co-ordinate economic, foreign and social policies in the 14 member states dominated by former British colonies.

Top: *scattered cays in the Grenadine islands*
Above: *a smiling face from Antigua*

People

Few of the Caribbean's original Amerindian inhabitants survived the first century of European exploration, decimated through disease, warfare and forced labour. In their place it is estimated that some 40 million West African slaves were transported to the Caribbean in the largest forced migration of human beings in history. Their descendants form the majority of the Caribbean peoples, though a few Caribs have survived in Dominica and St Vincent, and Indians and South Americans have all added to the racial mix.

Essence of the Caribbean

An exotic medley of race, colour and creed, the diverse Caribbean heritage finds its expression in dozens of local festivals and events, most notably the annual Carnivals hosted by islands throughout the region.

Above: *a drummer beats time at the Junkanoo Festival on Grand Bahama*
Right: *revellers in Aruba*

From its 18th-century origins in the pre-Lenten masquerade balls of Trinidad's French Catholic planters, Carnival was hijacked by former slaves, infused with African folklore and rhythms, and transformed into a joyous celebration of freedom and independence. The fabulous costumes, parades, marching bands and non-stop dancing capture the exuberance of the Caribbean people, revealing the true essence of the Caribbean.

THE **10** ESSENTIALS

If you only have a short time to visit the Caribbean, or would like to get a really complete picture of the region, here are the essentials:

• **Beat crazy** – music is the heartbeat of the Caribbean. Among familiar reggae, dub, steel pan and calypso sounds, listen out also for *soca* (soul-calypso), *zouk* (French Antilles) and *merengue* (Dominican Republic).

• **Festivals and events** – grab any opportunity to join in local events from carnivals and calypso competitions to impromptu jump-ups (➤ 116).

• **Rum punch** – the ubiquitous Caribbean cocktail is served in virtually every bar.

• **Coral gardens** – a stunning submarine world of colourful corals and dazzling tropical fish awaits divers (➤ 112–13) and snorkellers.

• **Day sails** – the Caribbean is prime sailing territory. Some of the most beautiful day sails are around the British Virgin Islands (➤ 80) and St Vincent and the Grenadines (➤ 20).

• **Rainforest rambles** – take a break from the beach and hike into the luxuriant rainforest to sample yet another face of the Caribbean (➤ 12–13).

• **To market, to market** – the Caribbean's bustling markets offer local colour by the bucket load and it is difficult to leave without a bulging bag of ripe tropical fruits.

• **Coconut cooler** – fresh coconut milk drunk straight from the green nut is hard to beat. Roadside vendors lop the top off a fresh coconut and will teach first-timers to scoop out the jelly.

• **Shop 'til you drop** – the Caribbean offers great crafts buys, and the duty-free ports of Grand Cayman, Sint Maarten and St Thomas are a magnet for shoppers (➤ 104–8).

• **Get a tan** – however short your stay, treat the Caribbean sun with respect. Use high-factor sun protection, and remember you can burn even on cloudy days.

Above: *a refreshing rainforest swimming hole, Guadeloupe*

Rum punch is a Caribbean cocktail favourite best served with a sprinkling of nutmeg

The Shaping of the Caribbean

Christopher Columbus sets sail on another voyage of discovery from the fort of Santo Domingo on the newly claimed Spanish colony of Hispaniola (1494)

c1000 BC
Amerindian settlers migrate to the Caribbean islands from South America.

cAD 120
Arawak Indians, farmers and fishermen gradually spread through the region.

c800
Warlike Carib Indians begin to push the Arawaks from the Lesser Antilles.

1492
Christopher Columbus reaches the New World while searching for a western route to the East Indies. He names his discovery the West Indies.

1498–1500
Columbus's third voyage locates the Central American mainland, and a settlement is established on Hispaniola (Dominican Republic).

1502–4
Columbus's fourth (and final) voyage.

1600s
Spanish treasure ships are targeted during the 'Golden Age' of Caribbean piracy. Sugar-cane is introduced and African slaves are transported to work the plantations.

1623
The first English colony is established on St Kitts.

1634–5
The Dutch take Curaçao from Spain; the French settle Guadeloupe and Martinique.

1671
Denmark colonises St Thomas.

1756–63
Anglo-French conflict in the European Seven Years' War is mirrored in the Caribbean.

1814–15
European powers carve up the West Indies at the end of the Napoleonic Wars; Britain grabs the lion's share.

1834
The Emancipation Act abolishes slavery in Britain and her colonies, followed by the French (1848) and the Dutch (1863).

10

The Danes built Fort Christian in Charlotte Amalie, St Thomas

1917
The US purchases the Virgin Islands of St Croix, St John, and St Thomas from Denmark for US$25 million.

1959
Fidel Castro introduces Communism to Cuba.

1962
Cuban missile crisis. Jamaica becomes the first British colony to take Independence.

1983
Combined US–Eastern Caribbean 'friendly invasion' of Grenada ends a four-year socialist regime.

1994
US invasion of Haiti fails to resolve the country's on-going crisis.

1995
Hurricanes Luis and Marilyn cause damage.

1998
Puerto Ricans vote against US statehood.

The devastation caused by Hurricane Luis in 1995

Peace & Quiet

The scissor-tailed profile of the magnificent frigate bird, which has a wingspan that can measure up to 8ft (2.4m)

Eco-tourism is the new buzz word in the Caribbean, and it's great news for visitors keen to venture beyond the beach and experience the best of the region's alternative natural wonders. National parks in the Windward Islands, Guadeloupe and Puerto Rico preserve vast tracts of lush tropical rainforest. There is the desert-like *cunucu* backcountry of Aruba and Curaçao in the Dutch Leewards and coastal mangrove swamps of Trinidad where wetlands birds gather in their thousands. Local guide companies offer hiking, horse riding, birdwatching and kayaking adventures (➤ 110–11). Whale-watching is a possibility in winter, while summer season turtle-watching walks visit beaches where giant sea turtles come ashore to lay their eggs. For peace and quiet beneath the waves, divers are spoilt for choice. Some of the finest dive sites in the world can be found in the protected marine parks of Bonaire, the Cayman Islands, Dominica, St Lucia and Tobago (➤ 112–13).

An aerial view of palm ferns and dense greenery in St Lucia's rainforest

Rainforest

The richest natural habitat on the planet, true rainforest requires an annual rainfall in excess of 70 inches (178cm). Regularly watered by clouds carried on the Atlantic trade winds, the volcanic peaks of the Eastern Caribbean islands and mountainous highlands in the Western Caribbean are cloaked in a dense jungle of rain-forest foliage. At lower altitudes, massive mahogany, gommier and santinay trees form the rainforest canopy towering 100ft (30m) above the fern-carpeted forest floor. Sturdily buttressed to support their weight, the mighty tree trunks are entwined by ropes of liana and other climbing plants. Further up the mountain, tree branches are festooned with ferns, orchids and bromeliads in the montane or cloud forest, and higher still, in the cool and often misty elevations of the elfin forest, eerily stunted trees covered in mosses and lichens punctuate the grasslands.

The best way to experience the rainforest is in the company of a knowledgeable local guide. Wear comfortable, loose-fitting cotton clothes and sensible footwear as it can get muddy and slippery. Take a swimsuit if there is a mountain stream on the itinerary, and warm clothes or a water-proof for high-altitude hikes.

Wildlife

Caribbean fauna is quite limited, with only a handful of mammals such as opossums and agoutis making their home in the forest. Tree frogs, iguanas and dozens of smaller lizard species are native to the islands, as are several non-venomous snakes and the highly poisonous fer de

lance found on Martinique and St Lucia. The region's bird life is much more varied and exotic. Dominica, St Lucia and St Vincent all have rare parrots, Bonaire is famed for its flamingo colonies, and the evening flight of the scarlet ibis in Trinidad's Caroni Swamp is spectacular. More common sights are tiny jewel-like hummingbirds, honeycreepers and cheeky black and yellow bananaquits, fearless breakfast bandits who cannot resist a stab at the sugar bowl.

Glorious Gardens

The Caribbean islands are ablaze with the colourful blooms of tropical plants from bougainvillaea and hibiscus to flowering trees such as poinciana and poui. Botanical gardens are not only havens of peace and quiet, they also showcase the enormous variety of native and imported plants which flourish in the region. Many flower farms growing heliconias, gingers and other exotic plants for export also welcome visitors.

Top to bottom: *yellow orchid blooms; a watchful anoli lizard; the exotic red ginger flower*

The Caribbean's Famous

A Continuing Saga
Columbus's journeyings did not end with his death in the Spanish city of Valladolid. His remains were taken to Seville and later removed to Santo Domingo's cathedral in the Dominican Republic. When Santo Domingo was ceded to France in 1795, some remains were removed to Spanish soil in Cuba. However, another urn was discovered during repairs to the cathedral in 1877, and declared the 'true' remains. These have since been placed in the city's Faro a Colón (► 39).

Christopher Columbus

Born Cristoforo Columbo in the Italian port of Genoa, Christopher Columbus (1451–1506) led the European discovery of the New World. Little is known of his early career, but Columbus's conviction that he could reach the East Indian 'Spice Islands' by sailing west eventually led him to seek patronage from the court of Spain. He sailed with three ships on 3 August, 1492, and sighted the Bahama Islands on 12 October. In all he made four voyages to the Caribbean (► 10), but was replaced as Viceroy of the Indies for bad administration, and died an embittered man (► panel).

Sir Henry Morgan

During the Golden Age of Caribbean piracy, few looted and burned as comprehensively and yet retired as comfortably as the Welsh buccaneer Henry Morgan (1635–88). A member of the 1655 English expedition which seized Jamaica from Spain, Morgan plundered the Spanish Main with enthusiasm, but an untimely attack on Panama during a temporary Anglo-Spanish peace saw him transported back to London for punishment. Soon the old enemies were at war again, and Morgan was knighted by Charles II in 1672. He returned to Jamaica as deputy governor, and later retired to the life of a wealthy and respected planter.

Bob Marley

Nesta Robert Marley (1945–81), reggae's most enduring legend, was born in the country parish of St Ann's, Jamaica. Brought up by his mother, he would sing to customers in her grocery store as a small child, before moving to Kingston's Trenchtown ghetto in 1957. Marley achieved his first local recording success with the Wailing Wailers in 1964. A collaboration with veteran producer Lee Perry brought the Wailers to the attention of Island Records boss Chris Blackwell, who signed them up and arranged UK and US tours in 1973. Major international success arrived with *Natty Dread* (1975), featuring *No Woman No Cry*.

A dreadlocked Bob Marley in concert before his early death aged 36

Top Ten

Above: *a fishing boat on Grenada's Grand Anse beach*
Right: *souvenir carving from the Dominican Republic*

15

1
Blue Mountains, Jamaica

28B3

✉ Blue Mountain National
Park, Hollywell Park
Ranger Station, on the
B1 north of Newcastle

☎ (876) 977-8044

🕓 Open site

✋ Free

❓ Blue Mountain Bicycle
Ride ☎ (876) 974-7075
guides cyclists 15 miles
(24km) downhill on
mountain roads. Blue
Mountain Peak ascents,
rainforest hikes and
kayaking expeditions
can be arranged through
Sense Adventures,
Kingston ☎ (876) 927-
2097; Valley Hikes, Port
Antonio ☎ (876) 993-
3881, offer a number of
walks around the Rio
Grande valley

*Famous for their beauty and their coffee, the
towering peaks of the Blue Mountains soar majes-
tically skywards, shrouded in a smoky blue haze.*

Viewed from a distance, the second highest mountain
range in the Caribbean (after Pico Duarte in the Cordillera
Central, Dominican Republic) really is blue. Rising steeply
in forested folds above the coast, the Blue Mountains
dominate the eastern portion of the island, stretched
between the capital, Kingston, and Port Antonio. Five
major peaks are strung out along the Grand Ridge, culminating in Blue Mountain Peak (7,402ft/2,256m), where the
air is distinctly crisp and there are views stretching as far
as Cuba on a clear day.

A welcome escape from the heat and crowds on
Jamaica's popular beaches, the Blue Mountains make a
great day-trip drive. The main road across the mountains is
the A3 from Annotto Bay on the north coast to Kingston,
but the best scenic route is the B1 Buff Bay–Kingston road
via Newcastle. An alternative option for more energetic
types is a guided downhill bike ride (clients are transported
up the mountains). Hikers can strike off the beaten track
into the rainforest, where there are over 250 species of
bird to be spotted, giant
swallowtail butterflies flitting
by and cool mountain
streams to bathe in.

Above 3,000ft (915m)
coffee plantations cling to
the slopes. Mellow arabica
coffee beans, known as
cherries, are harvested by
hand between September
and February. This is the
best time to visit the coffee
estates such as Mavis Bank,
off the B1 (free tours daily).
Another favourite stop is the
Cinchona Gardens, originally
laid out as a plantation in
1868, with stunning views
near the mountain village
of Section.

*The Blue Mountain coffee-
producing centre of Mavis
Bank on the steep slopes
below the Grand Ridge*

2
Bonaire Marine Park, Bonaire

One of the world's top dive destinations, Bonaire is fringed by reefs harbouring more than 200 species of fish and 30 types of coral.

A green turtle paddles past an intricately patterned brain coral

Fifty miles (80km) off the coast of Venezuela, the pint-sized, cactus-strewn island of Bonaire is far removed from the usual notion of lush Caribbean loveliness. But its underwater scenery is quite another story, a dazzling submarine world of pristine corals and diverse marine life protected by the Bonaire Marine Park which extends right around the island and the neighbouring islet of Klein Bonaire out to the 200ft (60m) contour mark.

The park's best diving is off the sheltered west coast, where the water is calm and visibility averages 100ft (30m) or more throughout the year. From the shore, the seabed shelves gradually in a series of terraces through areas of elkhorn coral to patch reefs, where staghorn and alarmingly realistic brain corals flourish. Jewelfish, butterflyfish, angelfish, peacock flounders and tangs are among the colourful inhabitants of the coral reef. Schools of larger fish patrol the reef crest feeding off drifting plankton at the edge of the drop-off which plummets to depths of 150ft (45m) or more. The park has 80-plus dive sites to choose from, several of them walk-in sites, such as Thousand Steps, accessible from the shore.

An excellent guided snorkelling programme provides reef tours lead by experienced local guides to a dozen sites within the park.

✚ 29D2

✉ PO Box 368, Bonaire, Netherlands Antilles. The park headquarters are at Barcadera, 2 miles (3km) north of Kralendijk ☎ (5997) 8444; web: www.bmp.org

🕐 Open site

✋ Moderate annual fee payable at the park headquarters or to dive operators

❓ Diving and snorkelling equipment can be rented from local operators (➤ 112–13) and most hotels. There are strict laws forbidding spearfishing and the removal of anything living or dead (except rubbish) from the park

3
Grenada

Below: *nutmeg sorting*
Right: *cocoa pods,*
nutmeg and ginger root

Grenada is the Spice Island of the Caribbean,
redolent with the scents of nutmeg, cinnamon and
cloves sailors claim they can smell on the breeze.

 54B2

 Grenada Board of
Tourism, Burns Point, St
George's ☎ (473) 440-
2279; web:
www.grenada.org.
There is also an
information kiosk at the
cruise-ship jetty on the
Carenage

 Spice Island Jazz
Festival (May–Jun),
Carnival (Jul–Aug)

National Museum

 Monckton Street (off
Long Street), St
George's

 (473) 440-3725

 Mon–Fri 9–4:30, Sat
10:30–2

 Cheap

Dougaldston Estate

 South of Gouyave

☎ Mon–Fri 9–4, Sat 9–1

Cheap

At the southern extent of the Windward Islands, Grenada
possesses an alluring combination of rugged rainforest
highlands and a coastline dotted with secluded coves and
sandy beaches. The island was named by 16th-century
Spanish sailors homesick for the mountains of Granada,
but years of French and British influence changed the
pronunciation to *Grenayda*. In 1983, after nine years of
independence from Britain, a combined US–Eastern
Caribbean 'friendly invasion' stabilised the country after the
collapse of a left-wing government. Since then things have
been quiet and Grenada has developed into one of the
most relaxed and welcoming islands in the region.

The island capital, St George's, is nestled on the slopes
of an extinct volcanic crater. Behind the curving waterfront
Carenage, where cruise-ship passengers come ashore, old
Georgian buildings and pastel-coloured homes scale the
hillsides in a cat's cradle of narrow streets. The **National
Museum** is worth visiting for its archaeological and historic
artefacts, and there are great views of the town from Fort
George at the harbour mouth. For a real slice of Grenadian
life, check out the colourful spice and produce stalls on
Market Square (busiest on a Saturday).

A tour of the island is a 'must'. Starting from St
George's, head up the west coast and strike inland for
Concord Falls, a series of three waterfalls tumbling down
from Mount Qua Qua. The lowest is a favourite tourist
stop, but it is possible to escape the crowds by hiking up
to the higher falls and cooling off in freshwater pools.

Just south of the fishing village of Gouyave, the old

Dougaldston Estate spice processing station illustrates how spices were prepared in time-honoured (technology-free) fashion. In Gouyave itself, passers-by are welcome at the Grenada Nutmeg Cooperative to watch nutmegs being sorted, graded and packed into sacks for market.

On the north coast, Sauteurs has a grim historical connection. The name translates from French as 'leapers', and there is a section of sea cliffs behind the village known as Carib's Leap, where the last of Grenada's Carib Indians preferred to jump to their deaths rather than submit to French rule in 1651.

On the northeast coast, Levera National Park offers walking trails, beaches and snorkelling.

At Grenville, the cross-island road climbs up into the rainforest and the luxuriantly green heights of Grand Etang National Park. Several hiking trails depart from near the roadside park centre; alternatively, for a rather less rugged experience, stop off at the Annandale Falls, a pretty (and popular) waterfall and bathing pool on the road back to St George's.

South of St George's, Grenada's most developed beach is Grand Anse. Lined with a handful of low-rise hotels, it is a good place to find watersports and dive facilities. One of the nicest secluded beaches is La Sagesse, on the south coast, with excellent snorkelling and a small restaurant.

The Carenage waterfront on St George's Harbour

Grenada Nutmeg Cooperative

✉ Main Street, Gouyave

🕐 Mon–Sat 9–4

✋ Tip for the guide

Grand Etang National Park Centre

✉ Grand Etang

🕐 Mon–Sat 8–4, Sun for cruise visitors

✋ Free

Annandale Falls

✉ 7 miles (11km) northeast of St George's

🕐 Daily 9–4

✋ Cheap

4
The Grenadines

 54C2

See St Vincent (► 90)

Several inexpensive return ferry services (one hour) daily between St Vincent and Bequia. The M/V *Barracuda* mail boat sails from St Vincent to Bequia, Canouan, Mayreau and Union Island on Mon and Thu, returning on Tue and Fri; round-trip minus Bequia on Sat. For schedules and further information, contact the head office in Kingstown, St Vincent ☎ (784) 457-1502

Sailing yachts bring divers and latter-day Robinson Crusoes to the uninhabited Tobago Cays

This jewel-like chain of 30 or so tiny, tropical islands and uninhabited cays is a magnet for adventurous yachtspeople and divers.

The Grenadine Islands trail south in a gentle 70-mile-long (112km) arc from St Vincent towards Grenada. Only eight of the islands are inhabited, linked by a regular mail-boat service which also ferries passengers.

Lying 9 miles (14km) south of St Vincent, Bequia (pronounced Beck-wee) is the largest and most developed of the Grenadines. The main settlement of Port Elizabeth is an appealing huddle of clapboard buildings, craft shops and restaurants, with a water taxi service to Princess Margaret Beach and Lower Bay; at the north end of the island is a turtle sanctuary.

An hour's sail by private yacht from Bequia is chic Mustique. The island is run as a private company with an elegant hotel and villa rentals. Mere mortals are permitted to enjoy the beaches and Basil's Bar.

Quiet Canouan is ringed by superb beaches and reefs, and Grand Bay is a popular yachting anchorage. Tiny Mayreau also has lovely beaches on the leeward coast and a couple of friendly guest-house bars. Boats from Mayreau and Union Island sail to the Tobago Cays for exceptional coral reef diving. Union is the Grenadines' southern transport hub with connections to the island resorts of Palm Island and Petit St Vincent (better known as 'PSV').

5
Harrison's Cave, Barbados

Barbados's top visitor attraction reveals a stunning subterranean world of stalactites and stalagmites on tram tours of a limestone cave network.

✚	54C2
✉	Highway 2, St Thomas District
☎	(246) 438-6640
🕐	Tours daily 9–4
🍴	Snacks (£)
↔	Flower Forest (➤ 57)

Harrison's Cave was first recorded in 1796, though the underground cave complex remained relatively undisturbed until its rediscovery in 1970. A rarity in the Caribbean region, the network of caverns, rivers, waterfalls and pools burrows beneath the porous limestone crust of central Barbados for almost a mile. Its walls are crusted with glistening calcite flowstones and the roof is festooned with needle-sharp stalactites dripping like icicles on to the thicker posts of stalagmites growing up from the cave floor. Occasionally, the stalactites and stalagmites meet to form whole pillars and dozens of other speleotherms (cave formations) transform the caverns into a fairy-tale scene with the assistance of suitably theatrical lighting.

The cave's dramatic decorations began to form over half a million years ago. The speleotherms are caused by precipitation as rainwater enriched with carbon dioxide from the air filters through the limestone as a weak carbonic solution until it reaches the dry underground cavern and evaporates into solid calcite crystals. It's an immensely slow process, taking approximately 100 years to grow a single cubic inch of calcite, or several hundred thousand years to form a pillar.

The tram ride commences at the visitor centre and trundles down into the caves with stops along the way for photographs. The route follows the subterranean stream that first carved the cavern network from the limestone and ends up at a deep pool fed by a waterfall before returning to base. Near by, Welchman's Hall Gully is another popular beauty spot with a botanical walk laid out in a collapsed portion of the same cave system.

The still green waters in the illuminated underground caverns of Harrison's Cave

6
Nelson's Dockyard, Antigua

Below: *Lord Nelson*
Right: *coral stone pillars at the Admiral's Inn*

One of the most picturesque historic sites in the Caribbean, the world's only remaining Georgian dockyard complex has been restored.

➕ 54B4

✉ English Harbour

☎ (268) 460-1379

🕓 Dockyard and Shirley Heights, daily 8–6 (open sites/free admission outside these times); Dow's Hill Historical Centre, daily 9–5

🍴 Shirley Heights Lookout (£–££). In the dockyard, Admiral's Inn (£–££), Copper & Lumber Store (££–£££) and snacks from the Dockyard Bakery (£)

♿ Few

✋ Moderate joint admission to all sites

❓ Regular dockyard tours depart from the entrance during the day

Tucked into the sheltered confines of English Harbour on the south coast of Antigua is Nelson's Dockyard, renamed in honour of its most illustrious visitor, naval hero Admiral Lord Nelson, who was a mere captain during his tour of duty between 1784 and 1787. A noted hurricane hole (sheltered harbour offering protection from hurricanes) and the Eastern Caribbean headquarters of the British Royal Navy during the 17th and 18th centuries, English Harbour is an admirable anchorage in every way. The dockyard sits on the inner harbour, which can only be reached by a narrow channel guarded by Fort Berkeley, from where there are fine views. In addition, the bay and its approaches are overlooked by steep, scrub-covered hills where the ruins of the Shirley Heights garrison still bring the odd cannon to bear on invading yachtsmen.

Shirley Heights is a good place to begin an exploration of the national park with a visit to the Dow's Hill Historical Centre for a short multimedia show tracing Antiguan history and culture. Further up the hill, past scattered cactus-studded ruins, stop to admire the views from the Shirley Heights Lookout (▶ 71).

Down in the dockyard, the neat coral rock and wood Georgian buildings have been painstakingly restored. Informative signboards explain the function of the various old naval stores and workshops, such as the Pitch and Tar Store, which has been transformed into the Admiral's Inn with the pillars of an old sail loft in the garden. A small museum is housed in the Admiral's House, the last house to be built in the dockyard before it was abandoned in 1889, and a walking trail leads out to Fort Berkeley.

7
Nevis

Nevis's reputation for gracious hospitality dates back to the plantation era when the island was hailed as the 'Queen of the Caribbees'.

Almost free of clouds, Nevis Peak rises above the Old Manor Hotel

Nevis, the little sister island to neighbouring St Kitts, is a tiny volcanic blip climbing steeply through a tangle of rainforest to cloud-capped Nevis Peak (3,232ft/985m). The snowy clouds inspired Columbus to name the island Nuestra Señora de las Nieves (Our Lady of Snows), later changed to Nevis (pronounced Nee-vis). During the 17th and 18th centuries, Nevisian planters grew rich on profits from the sugar trade and a thriving slave market, enabling them to construct the lovely plantation houses, since transformed into hotels, which are Nevis's main draw today.

The island can be explored on a day trip, but the relaxed and friendly pace of the island is best experienced from the comfort of a plantation-era inn. Ferries from St Kitts arrive in the sleepy capital of Charlestown, strung out along a main street lined with faded West Indian ginger-bread buildings. At the northern entrance to town, the **Museum of Nevis** covers local history in Alexander Hamilton House, birthplace of the 18th-century American statesman whose portrait graces US$10 bills. Beyond, Pinney's Beach unfurls along the leeward coast in a 3-mile (5km) swath of golden sand.

East of Charlestown, the **Nelson Museum** exhibits historical displays and souvenirs dedicated to Lord Nelson (► 22), and an impressive Botanical Garden overlooks the south coast from the grounds of the Montpelier Estate, where Nelson married local girl Fanny Nesbit in 1787. Montpelier and another three of Nevis's five plantation house hotels are located near by in the pretty Gingerland and Fig Tree Village districts. The Hermitage makes a great lunch stop.

✚ 54B4

🛈 Independence Square, Main Street, Charlestown ☎ (869) 469-1042

⛴ Round-trip ferry services from St Kitts Mon, Wed, Fri–Sat

Museum of Nevis

✉ Low Street, Charlestown

☎ (869) 469-5786

🕒 Mon–Fri 8–4, Sat 9–12

✋ Cheap

Nelson Museum

✉ Bath Road

☎ (869) 469-0408

🕒 Mon–Fri 9–4, Sat 10–2

✋ Cheap

8
Parc National de la Guadeloupe

✝ 54B4

✉ Basse-Terre

🕐 Open site

✋ Free

❓ Guided hikes arranged through the Bureau des Guides de Moyenne Montagne ☎ (590) 81-24-83, and Les Amis du Parc National ☎ (590) 81-45-53

Maison du Volcan

🕐 Daily 10–6

✋ Free

The Chutes du Carbet plummet down the lush slopes of La Soufrière

Carib Indians called Guadeloupe Karukera (Island of Beautiful Waters), and it certainly lives up to its name in this magnificent national park.

Literally thousands of rivulets and streams course down the flanks of Guadeloupe's central mountain range, feeding glassy calm lakes and dozens of waterfalls cascading into deep fern-edged pools. Generously replenished by an average annual rainfall of 250in (635cm), water is a constant presence in the highland rainforest of Guadeloupe. Here on Basse-Terre, the western wing of the island, the national park extends over 74,000 acres (30,000ha) incorporating 190 miles (305km) of hiking trails, tranquil beauty spots, bubbling hot springs and the smouldering bulk of La Soufrière (4,813ft/1,467m), an active volcano and the highest point in the Eastern Caribbean.

There are three main access points to the national park. The Maison de la Fôret, on the cross-island Route de la Traversée (▶ 62), is the starting point for several short walks and longer trails into the rainforest. South of Capesterre, on the east coast, side roads strike into the hills for the Chutes du Carbet, a series of three waterfalls. The most popular of these is the 360ft (110m) second fall, a 20-minute hike from the parking area; the 410ft (125m) upper cascade can only be reached by a challenging two-hour uphill climb.

Above the town of Basse-Terre the D11 winds up to the **Maison du Volcan** for an introduction to La Soufrière. The road ends at Savane à Mulets, 1,000ft (305m) from the summit. The round-trip hike takes around 2½ hours on a well-marked trail past old lava flows and sludge deposited during La Soufrière's most recent eruption in 1976. At the summit, a chain of smelly sulphur pits steams in the mist and the ground radiates heat.

9
St John,
US Virgin Islands

Two-thirds of St John, the unspoilt gem of the US Virgin Islands, is protected by a national park which extends into an offshore marine preserve.

Pleasure boats gather in the sheltered confines of Cruz Bay

Just 2 miles (3km) across the Pillsbury Sound from St Thomas (➤ 84), the rugged, green outline of St John promises a welcome respite from the upbeat bustle and crowds of its more developed sister island. The only way to reach St John is by boat, so the short sea crossing itself sets the tone for the island's relaxed charm, reinforced by the grid of tiny streets and clapboard buildings that greet visitors on the dockside at Cruz Bay, the main settlement.

Plantations once carpeted St John with sugar-cane. More than 100 small plantations have now been overrun by the forest, though visitors can still explore the ruins of the Annaberg Plantation, which is part of the **Virgin Islands National Park**. The park headquarters in Cruz Bay are a good place to plan an exploration of the island. Alongside historical and natural history displays, maps detail the park's 22 trails, ranging from short strolls out of Cruz Bay to longer hikes in the hills. Park rangers organise a varied programme of activities. A favourite is the guided 2½-mile (4km) Reef Bay Trail (check schedules).

St John's best beaches are on the north coast; Trunk Bay has a popular snorkelling trail in the national park's marine preserve. Other options include Hawksnest Beach, Cinnamon and Maho Bays. No tour would be complete without a drive along Centerline Road, with superb views across Drake's Passage to the British Virgin Islands.

54A5

St John Tourist Office, Cruz Bay ☎ (340) 776-6450

Restaurants and cafés (£–£££)

Frequent ferry services between St Thomas and Cruz Bay during the day (45 minutes from Charlotte Amalie or 20 from Red Hook); check evening schedules

Virgin Islands National Park

Visitors' Center, Cruz Bay

☎ (340) 776-6201

Daily 8–4:30

Free. Inexpensive joint admission charge for Annaberg Historic Sugar Mill Ruins and Trunk Bay daily 8:30–3:30

10
San Juan Old Town, Puerto Rico

Below: *a stone* garita
Right: *quiet, cobbled streets in Old San Juan*

The lively and charming old Spanish quarter of San Juan has been miraculously preserved behind the battlements of its hulking colonial fortresses.

 29E3

 Wide selection of restaurants, cafés and bars (£–£££)

 Free trolley buses make frequent narrated circuits of the Old Town. There are trolley stops outside the bus terminal and near the cruise ship pier, or look for the yellow Parada signs

San Felipe del Morro

✉ Punta del Morro

☎ (787) 729-6960

🕐 Daily 9:15–5

 Cheap

Casa Blanca

✉ Calle San Sebastián 1

☎ (787) 724-4102

🕐 Tue–Sat 9–12, 1–4:30

Cheap

Founded in 1520 on the tip of the peninsula dividing San Juan Bay from the Atlantic, the old city of San Juan was the original *puerto rico* (rich port). The seven-block Old Town district is a living reminder of Puerto Rico's Spanish colonial history, largely restored to its 18th-century appearance. One of its chief charms is exploring the steep, narrow streets, often paved with bluish bricks brought out to the Caribbean as ballast on sailing ships, and discovering quiet *escalinatas* (step streets) lined by pastel-painted town houses adorned with wrought-iron balconies and flower-filled window boxes.

Old San Juan's top sightseeing attraction is the 16th-century fortress of **San Felipe del Morro**, a vast weather-beaten citadel with walls up to 20ft (6m) thick in places and views past the *garitas* (stone sentry posts) of the fortified headland to Fort San Cristóbal. Plaza de San José is a pretty spot with a statue of the Spanish explorer and discoverer of Florida, Juan Ponce de León, outside the 16th-century church where his family worshipped. Ponce de León's remains were finally interred a short walk downhill in the cathedral. His daughter and son-in-law's home, **Casa Blanca**, dates from 1521 and now contains a fascinating small museum of family life.

Old San Juan's busiest shopping streets are Calle Fortaleza and Calle San Francisco. To escape the bustle, take a stroll around the city walls on tree-lined Paseo de la Princesa, past the Raices Fountain, and along the waterfront to the monumental city gate at Puerta de San Juan.

What to See

Above: a flock of
hand-painted parrots
make a colourful
display
Right: making
music with a
steel-pan band,
Barbados

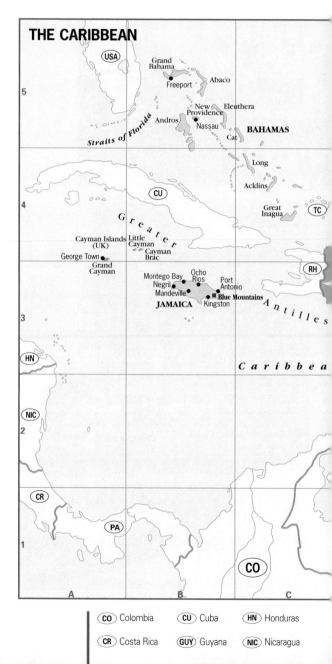

THE CARIBBEAN

USA

Grand Bahama
Freeport
Abaco
New Providence
Eleuthera
Andros
Nassau
Cat
BAHAMAS
Straits of Florida

Long

Acklins

Great Inagua

TC

CU

G r e a t e r

Cayman Islands (UK)
George Town
Little Cayman
Cayman Brac
Grand Cayman

RH

Montego Bay
Ocho Rios
Negril
Port Antonio
Mandeville
Blue Mountains
JAMAICA
Kingston
A n t i l l e s

HN

C a r i b b e a

NIC

CR

PA

CO

A   B   C

| CO Colombia | CU Cuba | HN Honduras |
| CR Costa Rica | GUY Guyana | NIC Nicaragua |

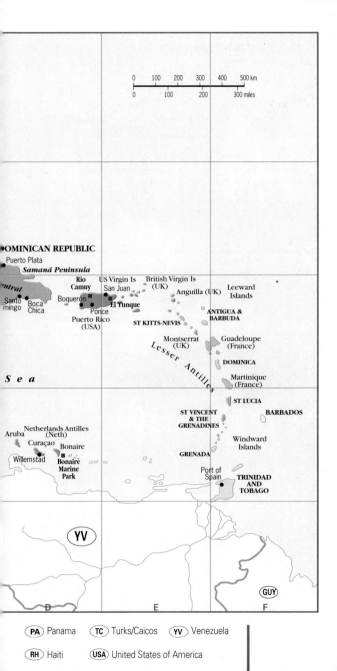

0   100   200   300   400   500 km
0   100   200   300 miles

DOMINICAN REPUBLIC
Puerto Plata
Samaná Peninsula
ntral
Santo   Río
mingo   Boca Camuy   US Virgin Is   British Virgin Is
        Chica Boquerón San Juan   (UK)   Leeward
                    El Yunque   Anguilla (UK)   Islands
              Ponce
        Puerto Rico   ANTIGUA &
          (USA)   ST KITTS-NEVIS   BARBUDA
                Montserrat   Guadeloupe
                  (UK)   (France)
          Lesser Antilles   DOMINICA

Sea   Martinique
                        (France)
                    ST LUCIA
              ST VINCENT   BARBADOS
  Netherlands Antilles & THE
Aruba   (Neth)   GRENADINES
    Curaçao   Windward
Willemstad   Bonaire   Islands
      Bonaire   GRENADA
      Marine
      Park   Port of
                    Spain   TRINIDAD
                          AND
                          TOBAGO

YV

GUY

D   E   F

PA Panama   TC Turks/Caicos   YV Venezuela

RH Haiti   USA United States of America

29

Western Caribbean

The Western Caribbean islands, stretching from the Yucatan Channel off Mexico east to Puerto Rico, form a natural barrier between the Atlantic Ocean and the northern extent of the Caribbean Sea. Generally known as the Greater Antilles, these islands are some of the largest in the region, packed with physical features ranging from spectacular mountain scenery and fine beaches to coastal plains and mangrove swamplands. In contrast to the Creole culture of the Eastern Caribbean, Western Caribbean islands such as the Dominican Republic retain strong links with their Spanish colonial history in language, architecture and religion. Puerto Rico may be an American territory, but its people are Spanish-speaking Catholics with a distinctive Latino flair. On the other hand, while Jamaica is a proudly independent cultural leader, proximity to the US has seen the Bahamas and Cayman Islands develop along unmistakably American lines.

' The West Indies I behold
Like the Hesperides of old –
Trees of life with fruits of gold. '

JAMES MONTGOMERY
A Voyage Round the World, Works
(1841)

———————•———————

Children at play in Freeport's International Bazaar, Grand Bahama

The Bahamas

Lying to the north of the true Caribbean islands, which encircle the Caribbean Sea, the 700 Bahama Islands (and several thousand more rocky islets and cays) appear 50 miles (80km) off the coast of Florida and stretch southeast for over 750 miles (1,200km). Only 30 of the islands are inhabited, with most of the population crowded on to the islands of Grand Bahama and New Providence, where the cruise-ship ports of Freeport and Nassau are among the busiest in the region.

Top: *sun and shade on Grand Bahama's Churchill Beach*
Above: *a pith-helmeted Bahamian policeman*

Christopher Columbus first sighted the New World in the Bahamas on 12 October, 1492, and the archipelago is named for the Spanish for 'shallow sea' (*baja mar*). British Puritans founded an early settlement on Eleuthera in 1648, before moving on to New Providence. The islands were a veritable pirates' lair in the 17th and 18th centuries, later providing a safe haven for Loyalists after the American War of Independence, Civil War gun-runners and Prohibition rum-runners. The Bahamas achieved independence from Britain in 1973, and although they remain part of the Commonwealth, the US influence is very strong. Tourism and offshore finance are the islands' chief revenue sources.

What to See in the Bahamas

GRAND BAHAMA ⭐⭐

The fourth largest of the Bahama Islands, measuring 96 miles (155km) from end to end, Grand Bahama made the leap from fishermen's backwater to international resort in a couple of decades during the 1950s and 1960s under the stewardship of American entrepreneur Wallace Groves. Both the island's main city, Freeport, and its beach resort annexe, Lucaya, were developed on the American model, with broad boulevards lined by high-rise hotels, US-style shopping malls and restaurants, and a glitzy nightlife featuring international cabarets and casinos. Grand Bahama's south coast is fringed by miles of pristine beaches, and there is excellent diving (➤ 112) and sport fishing in the area.

Bustling Freeport lives up to its name. This shopper's delight is well supplied with huge, air-conditioned malls crowded with holiday-makers in search of duty-free bargains. One of the top attractions in town is the **International Bazaar**, a 10-acre (4ha) open-air shopping complex which features eclectic architecture, stores piled high with luxury goods, and assorted local souvenirs for sale in the Straw Market. Port Lucaya is another favourite shopping, dining and entertainment spot, with a busy marina where glass-bottomed boat trips depart regularly for the offshore coral reefs.

On the eastern edge of Freeport, the **Garden of the Groves** was laid out in honour of Wallace Groves and his wife. The 12-acre (5ha) site is landscaped with exotic flowers and shrubs, palms trees, and pools fed by miniature waterfalls. Within the grounds, the Grand Bahama Museum traces local history and culture through displays of Lucayan Indian artefacts left by the island's original inhabitants, sections on pirates and marine life, and elaborate Junkanoo costumes worn during the annual winter season carnival.

The **Rand Memorial Nature Centre**, home to 21 species of wild orchids and a rich variety of birdlife including flamingos, is another pleasant retreat from the city streets, as is the Lucayan National Park, which has a network of trails carved through areas of scrub vegetation, forest and mangroves leading to a pair of limestone sinkholes.

✚ 28B5

🍴 Many dining and snack opportunities (£–£££)

🛈 Grand Bahama Tourist Office, PO Box F40251, International Bazaar, Freeport ☎ (242) 352-8044

❓ Junkanoo Carnival (Dec–Jan)

International Bazaar

✉ W Atlantic Drive (at W Sunrise Highway)

🕑 Mon–Sat 9–6

💲 Free

Shoppers take a break in the International Bazaar

Garden of the Groves

✉ Midshipman Road

☎ (242) 373-5668

🕑 Daily 9–4

💲 Gardens, cheap; museum, free

Rand Memorial Nature Centre

✉ East Settler's Way

☎ (242) 352-5438

🕑 Mon–Fri 9–4, Sat 9–1

💲 Moderate

❓ Guided tours. Also guided bird walk 1st Sat of month (8AM); wildflower walk 4th Sat of month (8AM)

A Walk around Nassau

Distance
2½ miles (4km)

Time
2 hours

Start/end point
Rawson Square

Lunch
Pick A Dilly at the Parliament
(£–££)
✉ 18 Parliament Street
(Parliament Square)
☎ (242) 322-2836

Nassau's attractive old town ranges uphill behind the waterfront and makes a pleasant stroll.

Start on Rawson Square, near the cruise-ship berth, where horse-drawn carriages wait under the trees.

Across Bay Street, the pink-and-white House of Assembly, the Ministry of Finance and the Supreme Court flank Parliament Square, overlooked by a statue of Queen Victoria.

Head west on Bay Street into the busy main shopping district, passing the touristy but fun Straw Market to 18th-century Vendue House, a former slave auction house facing George Street. Turn left.

Walking uphill on George Street, stop for a peek into the graceful interior of Christ Church Cathedral. At the top of the street, neo-classical Government House is the Governor-General's residence, also painted in Nassau's official ice-cream pink-and-white colour scheme.

Turn left on Duke Street, right on East Hill, and continue to the junction at East Street for a right and left turn on to Prison Lane.

A former lighthouse and look-out dating from 1793, Fort Fincastle looks like a tiny stone ship that has run aground on the hillside in the lee of the Water Tower. Both the fort and the 126-ft (38m) tower are open to visitors, the latter affording particularly panoramic harbour views.

Hunting for bargains in Nassau's bustling Straw Market is a popular pursuit with visitors

Take the Queen's Staircase down to Elizabeth Avenue. The 66 steps were hewn out of the limestone by 18th-century slaves.

On the corner of Shirley Street the Historical Society Museum illustrates local history with modest collections of artefacts, antique maps, paintings and photographs.

Elizabeth Street leads back down to Bay Street.

NEW PROVIDENCE ★★★

When the Puritan settlement on Eleuthera failed (► 32), its occupants relocated to a fine natural harbour on the island of New Providence and founded Nassau, the present-day capital of the Bahamas. At 21 miles by 7 miles (34km by 11km), New Providence is a fraction of the size of Grand Bahama, but it has far more to offer on the sight-seeing front and a colonial background more similar to its Caribbean neighbours.

Cruise ships literally queue up to spill their human cargo on to the Nassau dockside. The town's appealing old colonial heart is fun to explore (► Walk, opposite) and there are easy minibus connections to other sites around the island.

Heading west of town, **Fort Charlotte** was founded in 1788, and sprawls along the crest of a bluff. Guided tours scale the battlements and disappear into the dungeons. Near by, the tropical **Adastra Gardens** harbour a zoo full of monkeys, reptiles and birds, including the famous 'Marching Flamingos' (► 109). Hotel-lined Cable Beach is the island's resort headquarters fronting a magnificent sweep of sand with excellent watersports facilities and glass-bottomed boat trips. There are also bus and boat connections from Cable Beach and downtown Nassau to **Coral World**, a fascinating marine park boasting an under-water observatory, aquariums and a snorkel trail.

Linked to Nassau by a causeway, Paradise Island is another popular beach resort district with watersports and a golf course. Here, the lovely Versailles Gardens provide a quiet retreat landscaped with terraces and water features laid out around the 14th-century French cloisters imported from the pilgrim town of Lourdes in the 1960s.

✚ 28B5
🍽 Snack (£) and dining (£–£££) opportunities
ℹ Nassau Tourism & Development Board, PO Box N 5256, Nassau
☎ (242) 394-3575). Information kiosk at Rawson Square, Nassau
☎ (242) 326-9781)

Fort Charlotte
✉ Off West Bay Street
☎ (242) 325-9186
🕐 Mon–Sat 9–5
💷 Cheap

Adastra Gardens
✉ Chippingham Road
☎ (242) 323-5806
🕐 Daily 9–5
💷 Moderate
❓ Marching Flamingo shows daily at 11, 2 and 4

Coral World
✉ Silver Cay
☎ (242) 328-1036
🕐 Daily 9–6
💷 Moderate

Above: *the graceful Paradise Island Bridge spans Nassau Harbour*

Active beach-goers have a host of watersports to choose from on Seven Mile Beach, Grand Cayman

Cayman Islands

The Caymans, a trio of small, low-lying islands 150 miles (240km) south of Cuba, lie poised on the brink of the Cayman Trench, a 25,000ft (7,620m) trough at the deepest point of the Caribbean Sea. The dusty, scrub-covered islands are the tips of sea mountains, and although the landscape is uninspiring above sea-level, the Caymans offer spectacular underwater scenery with some of the finest diving in the world (➤ 112).

What to See in the Cayman Islands

GRAND CAYMAN ✪✪

Grand Cayman is the largest and most developed of the islands, and home to the Cayman Islands' capital, **George Town**. This offshore banking and insurance haven with a healthy tourist industry is a popular stop on cruise-ship itineraries, largely due to its tax-free shopping status. Shopping is a favourite pastime in downtown George Town, where Fort Street and the Kirk Freeport Plaza act as magnets for the shop-till-you-drop crowd. Walking-tour maps can be picked up from the quayside information kiosk, and the **Cayman Islands National Museum** is well worth investigating. Housed in the restored 1830s Old Courts Building, the museum provides an entertaining introduction to island history and traditions with an array of colonial artefacts, nautical memorabilia and in-depth sections on seafaring traditions and turtle-hunting.

Grand Cayman's tourist heartland is focused on the west coast of the peninsula north of George Town. Here, Seven Mile Beach (actually nearer 5½ miles/9km long) unfurls in a spectacular sweep of powder-soft white sand

fringed by hotels, condominiums, restaurants, bars and watersports centres offering windsurfer, jet-ski and sail boat rentals. (For a quiet beach, head for the island's East End or the snorkelling sites at Parrot's Reef and Smith's Cove, south of George Town.)

At the **Cayman Turtle Farm**, the world's only commercial green turtle farm, visitors are invited to observe the life cycle of a turtle from ping-pong ball-sized egg to 600lb (270kg) leviathan. A small proportion of the thousands of turtles bred here annually are released into the wild; others end up in the cooking pot and turtle cuisine can be sampled in the on-site café.

Inland from the turtle farm, the touristy enclave of Hell has sprouted a smattering of souvenir shops and a post office to compliment its curious collection of limestone rock formations. Postcards sell like hot cakes and get post-marked from Hell.

In the sheltered waters of North Sound, Stingray City offers an amazing opportunity to swim with wild but remarkably friendly stingrays. Some of these graceful creatures, which can measure up to 6ft (2m) from wingtip to wingtip, will nibble fishy snacks from the hand and allow themselves to be petted. There are boat trips, too. Non-divers can also survey the reefs aboard the **Atlantis Submarine**.

CAYMAN BRAC AND LITTLE CAYMAN

Life on these two diminutive islands, some 90 miles (145km) northeast of Grand Cayman (frequent local flights), is lived at a distinctly slower pace, and they make an ideal destination for a day-trip away from the crowds or a true escapist holiday. Both offer excellent diving and snorkelling, and bird-watchers are in for a treat with the Parrot Reserve on Cayman Brac, and Booby Pond Nature Reserve on Little Cayman.

Cayman Islands National Museum

✉ South Church Street at Shedden Road
☎ (345) 949-8368
🕓 Mon–Fri 9:30–5:30, Sat 10–4
💷 Cheap

Cayman Turtle Farm

✉ West Bay Road
☎ (345) 949-3894
🕓 Daily 9–5
🍴 Café (£)
💷 Moderate

Atlantis Submarine

✉ George Town Harbour
☎ (345) 949-7700
🕓 Mon–Sat 9–3
💷 Expensive

✚ 28B4

➕ 29D3

ℹ️ Secretariat de Estado de
Turismo, Bloque D,
Avenida México/30 de
Marzo, Apartado 497,
Santo Domingo,
República Dominicana
☎ (809) 221-4660; web:
www.codetel.net.do

❓ Carnival (pre-Lent)

Above: *an elegant
viceregal palace built for
Diego Columbus, the
waterfront Alcázar de
Colón dates from 1510*

✉️ South coast
🍴 Wide choice of cafés (£)
and restaurants (£–££)
ℹ️ ➤ above

Alcázar de Colón
✉️ La Atarazana
☎ (809) 687-5361
🕐 Wed–Mon 9–6
 Inexpensive

Dominican Republic

The second-largest country in the Caribbean (after Cuba), the Dominican Republic occupies two-thirds of the region's second-biggest island, Hispaniola, which it shares with Haiti. It also boasts the highest point in the Caribbean, Pico Duarte (10,417ft/3,175m) in the mountainous Cordillera Central, and the lowest at Lago Enriquillo, a briny lake 130ft (40m) below sea-level and home to crocodiles and flamingos. The Republic's 1,000-mile (1,600km) coastline, bordered by fabulous beaches, draws around two million tourists each year, mostly package holidaymakers who can enjoy a Caribbean holiday at comparatively low prices. However, there are a few problems in paradise. This is a very poor country, and visitors can expect a fair amount of hassle from hustlers around tourist complexes. The east end of the island and much of its tourist infrastructure was also hit badly by Hurricane Georges in 1998.

What to See in the Dominican Republic

SANTO DOMINGO ✪✪✪
Santo Domingo, the capital of the Dominican Republic, is the oldest city in the Americas, founded by Christopher Columbus's brother Bartolomeo in 1498 (Columbus himself first set foot in the New World on the north coast of Hispaniola in 1492). At the heart of the sprawling modern city, the Zona Colonial (Colonial Zone) has been miraculously preserved in a warren of narrow streets and gracious old stone buildings encircled by ancient walls. Here, Columbus's son, Don Diego, constructed the palatial **Alcázar de Colón**, one of the most impressive surviving

buildings from his term as viceroy. Its 22 rooms have been restored and furnished with 16th- to 17th-century antiques and tapestries. Near by, the **Museo de las Casas Reales** (Museum of the Royal Houses) displays notable collections of Amerindian and colonial artefacts including armour, weapons, maps and crafts in the 16th-century Governors Palace. The Renaissance Catedral de Santa Maria la Menor is another 'must see', with a fine art collection and an elaborate silver altar.

West of the Zona Colonial, Avenida George Washington is better known as the Malecón. This palm-lined seafront promenade is where the Dominicans make their evening *paseo* (stroll) to the strains of *merengue* music blasting from portable stereos.

To the east, across the River Ozama, the most striking landmark of the modern city is the vast **Faro a Colón** (Columbus Lighthouse), designed to commemorate the quincentenary of Columbus's arrival in 1992. As well as several museums, it houses lasers which imprint the night sky with a cross of light visible in Puerto Rico.

BOCA CHICA AND THE SOUTHEAST ✪✪

Twenty miles (32km) east of Santo Domingo, Boca Chica is the closest beach to the capital and one of the busiest on the island, particularly at weekends. A 20-minute drive further on, the soft, white palm-fringed sands around Juan Dolio are mercifully less crowded with just a couple of tourist hotels, while things hot up again at La Romana.

A short drive inland from La Romana, the artists' colony of Altos de Chavón occupies a picturesque spot above the River Chavón. This replica medieval Spanish village with pretty coral rock houses dripping bougainvillaea is a pleasant spot to while away an afternoon.

Museo de las Casas Reales
- ✉ Calle Las Damas
- ☎ (809) 682-4202
- 🕐 Tue–Sun 9–6
- 💰 Cheap

Faro a Colón
- ✉ Avenida España

➕ 29D3

A flourish of palm trees provide welcome shade on the beach at Boca Chica, east of Santo Domingo

 29D3

Above: *strolling in Puerto Plata's Central Park; the town is famous for its Victorian architecture*

 29D4
⊠ North coast
🍴 Cafés and restaurants (£–££)

Museo del Ambar
⊠ Calle Duarte 61
☎ (809) 586-2848
🕐 Mon–Sat 9–6
✋ Cheap

 29D4
⊠ North coast

CORDILLERA CENTRAL ✪✪
The island's dramatic central mountain range makes a great escape from the heat down on the coast. Nestled in the shadow of the high peaks, the hill towns of Constanza and Jarabacoa provide stops along the way. Keep an eye out for the Aguas Blancas waterfalls, 12 miles (19km) south of Constanza, and the Jimenoa falls near Jarabacoa.

PUERTO PLATA AND THE AMBER COAST ✪✪
Facing out on to the Atlantic, the 'Silver Port' was another early Spanish settlement. Still guarded by the hulking 16th-century citadel of Fortaleza San Felipe, it is a pleasant town with Creole gingerbread houses, tree-shaded plazas and the **Museo del Ambar** (Amber Museum) laid out in a charming town house. The Amber Coast is home to one of the world's largest amber deposits, and the most valuable pieces of this semiprecious fossilised pine resin contain *Jurassic Park*-style insects and plant fragments.

The best beaches lie to the east of town, stretching through the busy resort of Playa Dorada and lively but unpretentious Sousúa, to the windsurfers' favourite, Playa Cabarete.

SAMANÁ PENINSULA ✪✪✪
This lush and lovely peninsula juts out parallel to the north coast enclosing Samaná Bay. Las Terrenas, on the north shore, is arguably the nicest resort on the island, simple and laid-back with a great beach. The town of Samaná itself has little to recommend it, but there is terrific bird-watching in the mangrove swamps of the Los Haitises National Park to the east, and whale-watching is a top activity in the bay in the winter months (Dec–Feb).

Jamaica

Mountainous and beautiful Jamaica was called Xamayca (Land of Wood and Water) by Arawak Indians, while Columbus described it as 'the fairest island that eyes have beheld'. It is the third largest of the Caribbean islands at 4,411sq miles (11,420sq km), and its rich and varied terrain encompasses the heights of the Blue Mountains in the east (▶ 16), rugged Cockpit Country in the west, lush forests, rushing rivers and a necklace of superb north-coast beaches harbouring the main tourist areas of Montego Bay, Negril and Ocho Rios.

First settled by Spanish colonists in 1510, Jamaica was captured by the British in 1655, who transformed it into one of the world's largest and richest sugar producers. Jamaica was the first British colony to achieve full independence in 1962, and has played an important role in the development of regional culture as the birthplace of reggae and Rastafarianism.

What to See in Jamaica

KINGSTON ✪

Jamaica's capital, Kingston, is the least tourist-orientated town on the island, though there are several low-key sights to enjoy. One is a ferry ride across to the ruins of Fort Charles, the site of 17th-century Port Royal, a piratical hell-hole frequented by the likes of Henry Morgan and Edward Teach (aka Blackbeard) until it was destroyed during an earthquake in 1692.

✚ 28B3
🛈 Jamaica Tourist Board, PO Box 360, 2 St Lucia Avenue, Kingston 5 ☎ (876) 929-9200; web: www.jamaicatravel.com
❓ Reggae Sunsplash (Feb), Carnival (May)

Above: *tiny, verdant islands are strung out all along Jamaica's north coast; this one – Monkey Island – is off San San Beach near Port Antonio*

✉ South coast
🛈 See above

41

Above: *Devon House*
Right: *a wave runner cuts a dash on Montego Bay*

Bob Marley Museum

✉ 56 Hope Road
☎ (876) 927-9152
🕐 Mon–Fri 9:30–4:30
🏷 Cheap

✉ 50 miles (80km) west of Kingston

Stephenson Flower Garden
✉ Mandeville
☎ (876) 962-2909
🕐 Mon–Sat by appointment
🏷 Inexpensive

✉ North coast
🍴 Numerous dining options (£–£££)
ℹ Cornwall Beach ☎ (876) 952-4425

North of the downtown district, lovely Devon House, at 26 Hope Road, was built by George Stiebel, Jamaica's first black millionaire in 1881. The interior has been restored with antique furnishings and a collection of craft shops occupies the old stables.

Near by, the **Bob Marley Museum** honours the legendary Jamaican reggae star (▶ 14) with displays of memorabilia laid out in his former home and the Tuff Gong recording studio; and the Hope Botanical Gardens provide a blaze of colour in a 50-acre (20ha) public park with a small zoo.

MANDEVILLE ✪
Mandeville, a former British hill station, was established at a cool 2,000ft (610m) above the south coast in 1816, and has retained the slightly decorous air of a mountain resort and a clutch of fine Georgian buildings. Plant lovers should find time to visit the **Stephenson Flower Garden**, where Carmen Stephenson cultivates hundreds of rare orchids, anthuriums and fruit trees in her private garden.

MONTEGO BAY AND SURROUNDINGS ✪✪✪
Jamaica's tourist capital, MoBay (as it is generally known) is also the island's second-largest town and a popular cruise-ship destination. The city centre is Sam Sharpe Square, named after the leader of the 1831 slave rebellion whose statue watches over an assortment of street vendors stalls and The Cage, a former slave lock-up. Towards the waterfront there is fine souvenir-hunting at the busy Craft Market, while the main shopping and entertainment district lies to the north, focused on hotel-lined Gloucester Avenue. MoBay's resort pedigree dates back to the early 1900s when the widely touted restorative properties of sea bathing brought tourists to the sandy strand of Doctor's Cave Beach, the most popular beach in

town. Cornwall Beach is another good spot with watersports facilities.

MoBay is a good base for a variety of excursions. Due south of town, in the forested highlands above the village of Anchovy, 'bird lady' Lisa Salmon set up a bird feeding station in 1952. Today, the **Rockland Bird Sanctuary** offers a fascinating opportunity to view Jamaica's bird life close up. Dozens of native and migrating birds drop in for an afternoon snack and some, such as red-billed streamertails, the tiny hummingbirds known as doctor birds (Jamaica's national symbol), will feed from hand-held bottles of sugar water.

Heading east along the coast, **Rose Hall Great House** is the grandest of Jamaica's great houses, built around 1770 and furnished with antiques. Despite the opulent surroundings, the main topic of the guided tours is the legend of Annie Palmer, the so-called White Witch of Rose Hall. This infamous 19th-century mistress of the house is said to have murdered three husbands and a string of slave lovers before meeting her own gory end.

On a more cheerful note, the **Greenwood Great House** was built as a guest house by prosperous sugar planter relatives of the poet Elizabeth Barrett Browning. The sturdy grey stone mansion dates from the 1790s and its splendidly restored interior has been filled with antiques, rare books and a collection of unusual musical instruments. Another highlight of a visit here is the stupendous view across the estate to the sea from the upper-storey veranda.

Two miles (3km) inland from Falmouth, **Rafter's Village** is the start point for rafting trips on the Martha Brae River. Two-seater bamboo rafts poled by local guides make the lazy 90-minute journey downriver past unspoilt tropical jungle alive with birds and fluttering butterflies.

Above: *feeding time at Rockland Bird Sanctuary*

Rockland Bird Sanctuary
- ✉ Rockland, 9 miles (14km) south of Montego Bay
- ☎ (876) 952-2009
- ⏱ Daily 2–5
- ✋ Moderate

Rose Hall Great House
- ✉ 8 miles (13km) east of Montego Bay
- ☎ (876) 953-2323
- ⏱ Daily 9:30–6
- ✋ Expensive

Greenwood Great House
- ✉ 16 miles (25km) east of Montego Bay
- ☎ (876) 953-1077
- ⏱ Daily 9–6
- ✋ Moderate

Rafter's Village
- ✉ Falmouth
- ☎ (876) 954-5168
- ⏱ Raft trips daily 9–5
- ✋ Expensive (lunch and transfers included)

The art of relaxation: afloat in a calm cove sheltered by Negril's low cliffs

 West coast
Good selection of cafés and restaurants (£–£££)
Coral Seas Plaza ☎ (876) 957-4243

NEGRIL ✪✪✪

The laidback resort town of Negril, a former pirate haunt and 1960s hippy hang-out at the western tip of the island, is by far the most appealing tourist centre and boasts Jamaica's best beaches. Seven Mile Beach is the centre of the action, an impressive ribbon of palm-backed, talcum powder-soft sand running into low cliffs at the West End. The cliffs are overlooked by the 19th-century Negril Lighthouse. At the opposite end of the main beach, Bloody Bay caters to the 'clothing optional' crowd on the sands where whalers once cleaned their catch.

 North coast
Wide choice of dining options (£–£££)
Ocean Village Shopping Centre ☎ (876) 974-2582

Coyaba Gardens and Museum
Shaw Park Estate (off the A3)
☎ (876) 974-6235
Daily 8:30–5
Snacks (£)
Cheap

Shaw Park Gardens
Shaw Park Estate (off the A3)
☎ (876) 974-2723
Daily 8–5
Cheap

OCHO RIOS AND SURROUNDINGS ✪✪

A modern resort centre and Jamaica's chief cruise port, Ochi (in local parlance) is short on island charm but well supplied with all the tourist necessities, from great beaches and watersports to shopping, dining and nightlife. Above the city centre two lovely gardens offer a peaceful escape from the downtown bustle. The **Coyaba Gardens and Museum** doubles as a showcase for exotic tropical plantings and island history displays. Exhibits trace Jamaica's cross-cultural influences from the Arawak Indians (*coyaba* means 'paradise' in Arawak) through the plantation era to post-emancipation days. Next door, the glorious **Shaw Park Gardens** clamber across the hillside past cascading waterfalls, hibiscus, heliconias, gingers, crotons and red-hot catstails, with the additional benefit of magnificent views out to sea. A popular detour and botanical curio further up the road to Kingston is Fern Gully, a 3-mile (5km) stretch of road flanked by forest ferns and vines planted in a narrow chasm to create a sun-dappled tunnel of greenery.

Just west of Ocho Rios, the **Dunn's River Falls** are a top island attraction. These deliciously cool mountain waterfalls tumble down a series of ledges for 600ft (180m) through the forest to the coast. Sure-footed guides lead 'daisy chains' of swimsuited visitors hand-in-hand up the slippery route to the top. There are changing rooms and lockers down on the beach.

Travelling east along the coast, **Prospect Plantation** makes an interesting stop. The 1,000-acre (405ha) working plantation produces bananas, coffee, cocoa, pineapples, coconuts, limes and spices, and wagon trips run around the estate to the sugar-cane fields and a dramatic look-out above the White River Gorge. Horse-riding excursions are available, too.

Two of Jamaica's most famous expatriate residents built houses on the north coast. Playwright and composer Noel Coward's clifftop retreat, **Firefly**, has been meticulously restored with personal memorabilia including manuscripts, celebrity photographs and even his silk pyjamas. Coward's grave in the garden enjoys a panoramic view, 1,000ft (305m) above the sea. Ian Fleming, author of the *James Bond* books, made his winter home at Goldeneye, on the beachfront at Oracabessa, which served as a location for the first Bond film, *Dr No* (1962).

A 'daisy chain' of holidaymakers begins the ascent of Dunn's River Falls on Jamaica's north coast

Dunn's River Falls
- ✉ A1, 2 miles (3km) west of Ocho Rios
- ☎ (876) 974-2857
- 🕐 Daily 8–5
- 👣 Moderate

Prospect Plantation
- ✉ Off the A3, 4 miles (6km) east of Ocho Rios
- ☎ (876) 974-2058
- 🕐 Daily for tours at 10:30, 2, 3:30
- 👣 Expensive

Firefly
- ✉ Grants Pen, 2 miles (3km) south of Port Maria
- ☎ (876) 997-7201
- 🕐 Mon–Sat 9–4
- 🍴 Afternoon tea (£)
- 👣 Expensive

DID YOU KNOW?

The author Ian Fleming wrote 14 *James Bond* novels in Jamaica and named his 007 hero after the author of the classic Caribbean ornithological guide *Birds of the West Indies*.

45

✉ Northeast coast
ℹ City Centre Plaza
  ☎ (876) 993-3051

Nonsuch Caves and the Gardens of Athenry
✉ Nonsuch, 2 miles (3km) southeast of Port Antonio
☎ (876) 993-3740
🕐 Daily 9–4
💲 Inexpensive

YS Falls
✉ North of Middle Quarters (off the A2)
🕐 Tue–Sun 9:30–3:30
💲 Moderate

Appleton Estate Rum Tour
✉ B6, west of Siloah
☎ (876) 963-9215
🕐 Mon–Fri 9–4
💲 Expensive

A safari boat heads into the coastal swamplands of the Great Morass in search of crocodiles and birdlife

PORT ANTONIO ⭐

Blessed by not one, but two stunning deepwater bays and backed by the Blue Mountains, Port Antonio was a banana boat port and Jamaica's first resort around the turn of the 20th century. During the 1940s and 1950s it enjoyed a brief heyday as an exclusive Hollywood hideaway for the likes of Errol Flynn (who bought offshore Navy Island) and Bette Davis. Today, the town is mercifully undeveloped, a quiet oasis with a smattering of Victorian buildings. Nearby sights include the turquoise waters of the Blue Hole, the **Nonsuch Caves and the Gardens of Athenry**, and rafting on the Rio Grande.

THE SOUTHWEST ⭐⭐

Travelling west from Kingston, this is a quiet, undeveloped corner of the island somewhat off the beaten track. Twelve miles (19km) west of the city, the main road runs through historic Spanish Town, Jamaica's capital until 1872, and up into the mountains for Mandeville (➤ 42). Side roads run parallel to the coast past fishing villages, the clifftop look-out of Lover's Leap and the delightful seaside resort of Treasure Beach. At Black River, there are safari boat rides into the Great Morass swamp (➤ 110–11), which can be combined with a trip to the delectable **YS Falls**, a series of seven cascades reached by wagon rides across a working plantation.

In the hills above the coast, one of Jamaica's top visitor attractions is the **Appleton Estate Rum Tour**. Founded in 1749, Appleton is Jamaica's biggest and oldest rum enterprise, and distillery tours are rounded off with tastings of the local brew.

Puerto Rico

Puerto Rico is the most easterly and smallest of the main Greater Antillean islands, dominated by the rainforest-cloaked mountains of the Cordillera Central and fringed by beaches. The island was first settled by Spanish explorer Ponce de León in 1508, and held by Spain for four centuries before passing to the US after the 1898 Spanish-American War. Puerto Rico is a commonwealth territory of the US, and in recent years, despite energetic canvassing by the pro-US lobby, Puerto Ricans have so far rejected attempts to have their country adopted as the 51st State of the Union. The American influence is unavoidable in tourist areas, where both Spanish and English are commonly spoken, but the island's Spanish Catholic heritage is still widely evident in its fine colonial architecture, Spanish-style *fiestas*, Hispanic cuisine, and even the time-honoured evening *paseo* (a pre-dinner stroll).

What to See in Puerto Rico

SAN JUAN ✪✪✪
From modest colonial origins, San Juan has exploded into a sprawling modern city around San Juan Bay. The biggest draw here is the utterly charming Old Town (➤ 26). Most visitors stay in the modern Atlantic coast beach suburbs of Condado or Isla Verde, heading back into the Old Town for shopping and atmospheric dining in one of the cosy Spanish-style *bodegas*.

29D3

Puerto Rico Tourism Company Information, La Casita, Paseo de la Princesa (near Pier One), Old San Juan 00901
☎ (787) 722-1709; web: www.discoverpuertorico.com

Christmas celebrations culminate in Three Kings Day (6 Jan)

Above: *the high-rise hotels of Condado and Isla Verde back miles of sandy Atlantic beaches in San Juan*

✉ North coast
🍴 Numerous cafés and restaurants (£–£££)
ℹ ➤ above

Bacardi Rum Plant
- ✉ Route 888, Cataño
- ☎ (787) 788-1500
- 🕐 Mon–Sat 9–10:30, 12–4
- ✋ Free

✉ Southwest coast

Cabo Rojo Wildlife Refuge
- ✉ Rte 301 (KM5.1), Cabo Rojo
- ☎ (787) 851-7251
- 🕐 Mon–Fri 7:30–4
- ✋ Free

- ✉ Rte 3, 30 miles (48km) east of San Juan
- 🍴 Snack stands (£)

- ✉ South coast
- 🍴 Choice of cafés and restaurants (£–££)
- ℹ Plaza Las Delicias
  - ☎ (787) 840-5695

Museo Castillo Serrallés
- ✉ El Vigia Hill 17
- ☎ (787) 259-1774
- 🕐 Tue–Thu 9:30–4:30, Fri–Sun 10–5
- 🍴 Café (£)
- ✋ Cheap

A popular outing across the bay is a ferry ride from the Old Town (Pier Two) to the **Bacardi Rum Plant**, with great harbourside views. Tours take you inside the giant distillery, the bottling plant and a small museum of rum lore before freshening up with a free daiquiri.

BOQUERÓN ✪
In the far southwestern corner of the island, Boquerón is one of several small seaside resorts with great beaches and a relaxed air. This particularly splendid sweep of sand backed by palm trees is very popular at weekends. There are cafés and cabin rentals in the village, watersports equipment hire on the beach, and the **Cabo Rojo Wildlife Refuge** in the coastal mangrove forest to the south is home to waterfowl and wading birds.

LUQUILLO BEACH ✪✪
Luquillo, a magnificent mile-long crescent of sand on the Atlantic coast lapped by glassy turquoise water, is a favourite detour on the return trip from El Yunque (► opposite). There are windsurfer rentals and other watersports, and there is no need to bring a picnic as food stalls under the palm trees do a brisk trade in mouth-watering soft taco rolls stuffed with crab or lobster, *alcapurrias* (banana fritters), iced piña coladas and other temptations.

PONCE ✪✪
Puerto Rico's second city was founded by Ponce de León's great-grandson in the late 17th century. Its heart is tree-shaded Plaza las Delicias, flanked by the neo-classical Catedral Nuestra Señora de la Guadalupe and the eye-catching black and red-striped Parque de Bombas (fire station) dating from 1882. There are terrific views over Ponce from the 100-foot-tall (30m) observation tower on El Vigía Hill. Near by, the **Museo Castillo Serrallés** combines collections of family heirlooms, furnishings and a section on the history of rum in an imposing Spanish Revival mansion, with lovely gardens built for the wealthy rum-making Serrallés family in the 1930s.

An operational fire station until 1990, the Parque de Bombas now houses a fire-fighting museum

North of Ponce, the **Hacienda Buena Vista,** an old coffee estate, has been meticulously restored and is now a small museum which illustrates life on a working coffee plantation at the end of the 19th century. Tours visit the old estate house, former slave quarters and the corn and coffee mills which are operated by the original water-powered machinery.

Hacienda Buena Vista
- ✉ Rte 10 (KM16.8)
- ☎ Mon–Fri (787) 722-5882, Sat–Sun (787) 848-7020
- ⓘ By reservation, Fri–Sun
- 💰 Cheap

RÍO CAMUY CAVE PARK ✪✪
In the karst limestone hills of the Central West, the River Camuy has hollowed out a massive subterranean cave system that extends over 300 acres (120ha) making it one of the largest in the Americas. Tram tours go down a sinkhole to the mouth of the Clara Cave where a footpath picks up the trail into an impressive 170ft-high (52m) cavern festooned with towering stalagmites and giant icicle-like stalactites. Trams also tackle the 400ft-deep (120m) Tres Pueblos sinkhole for views of the Camuy.

- ✉ Rte 129 (KM18.9)
- ☎ (787) 898-3100
- ⓘ Wed–Sun 8–4
- 🍴 Café (£)
- 💰 Moderate

EL YUNQUE ✪✪✪
(CARIBBEAN NATIONAL FOREST)
On average it rains 350 days of the year (more than 100 billion gallons of rainwater annually) in Puerto Rico's lush and spectacular rainforest jungle. Some 2,000ft (610m) above sea-level, El Yunque (The Anvil) is a rampant tangle of lianas, ferns and epiphytes crowned by 100ft-tall (30m) trees and giant stooks of bamboo. Various trails depart from the visitor centre. The rare Puerto Rican parrot is still found here; look for its brilliant green and blue plumage and red head markings. Listen for the tiny, bright green tree frogs known as *coqui* after the 'ko-kee' sound of the males' strident mating call.

- ✉ El Portal Tropical Forest Center, Rte 191 (north of Rio Grande)
- ☎ (787) 888-1810
- ⓘ Forest, Mon–Fri 7:30–5, Sat–Sun 7:30–6; Forest Center, daily 9–5
- 💰 Forest, free. Forest Center, cheap

A mountain torrent rushes through El Yunque Caribbean National Forest

In the Know

If you only have a short time to visit the Caribbean, or would like to get a real flavour of the region, here are some ideas:

Grand Bahama's miles of sandy beaches are typical of the Caribbean Islands' main attraction

10
Ways to Be a Local

Relaaax – nothing, but nothing, happens fast in the Caribbean.

Haggle in the market for fresh tropical fruits, straw hats and spices.

Drink fresh coconut milk straight from the nut topped by a machete-wielding stallholder.

Limin' is the gentle art of idle chat best practised in the shade with a cold beer.

Rum and beer are produced on a host of islands. Check out the local brew.

Ride the bus – dollar buses are a cheap and easy way to get around, with a pumping dub or reggae soundtrack thrown in.

Honk your horn at every turn when driving around the islands.

Hike in Toyotas – the local nickname for plastic sandals bought for a few dollars in the market.

Wave at pedestrians and watch out for wandering livestock.

Wrap up off the beach – skimpy swimwear is not appreciated in town.

10
Best Beaches

Baie Longue, St Martin (65)
Dark Wood Beach, Antigua (► 71)
Eagle Beach and Palm Beach, Aruba (► 74)
Grande Anse des Salines, Martinique (► 64)
Magens Bay, St Thomas, USVI (► 84)
Negril, Jamaica (► 44)
Playa Dorada, Dominican Republic (► 40)
Shoal Bay, Anguilla (► 68)
Trunk Bay, St John, USVI (► 25)
The Baths, Virgin Gorda, BVI (► 81)

10
Best Beach Bars

Bar Fredo, Petite Anse d'Arlet, Martinique (► 64)
Bomba's, Paynes Bay (Holetown), Barbados (► 58)
Bomba's Shack, Apple Bay, Tortola, BVI (► 81)
Doolittle's, Marigot Bay, St Lucia (► 88)
Foxy's, Jost van Dyke, BVI (80)
Gorgeous Scilly Cay, Anguilla (► 68)
La Sagesse, Grenada (► 19)
Pigeon Point Beach Bar, Pigeon Point, Tobago (► 79)
Theresa's, Lower Bay, Bequia (► 20)
Turtle Beach Bar, Turtle Beach, St Kitts (► 73)

10
Top Activities

Birdwatching: top twitching opportunities at Rockland Bird Sanctuary, Jamaica (➤ 43), and Asa Wright Nature Centre and Caroni Bird Sanctuary, Trinidad (➤ 79).
Diving (➤ 112–13).
Mini-submarine rides: check out the coral reefs without getting wet in Grand Cayman (➤ 37) and St Thomas (➤ 84). Also Aruba, Barbados and New Providence (Bahamas).
Rainforest hikes: get off the beaten track in Jamaica's Blue Mountains (➤ 16), Guadeloupe (➤ 24), St Lucia (➤ 111) and St Vincent (➤ 111) among others.
Riding: is a great way to explore the Dutch ABCs' desert-like *cunucu* backcountry (➤ 111) or the rainforest heights of Nevis (➤ 23).

Shark-feeding is a job for the experts, but Caribbean diving and snorkelling is open to all

River-rafting: the cool way to explore Jamaica's Martha Brae (➤ 43) and Rio Grande (➤ 46) rivers.
Sailing: day sails with lunch and snorkelling are offered on most islands. Antigua (➤ 69) is a top yachting destination, but the best scenery is found in the British Virgin Islands (➤ 80) and the Grenadines (➤ 20).
Sportfishing: sailfish, marlin, wahoo and tuna are specialities of the Bahamas (➤ 32), Puerto Rico (➤ 47) and the Virgin Islands (➤ 80). Also bone-fishing in the Bahamas and the Cayman Islands (➤ 36).
Whale-watching: winter season whale- and dolphin-watching tours operate from several islands including the Dominican Republic (➤ 38–40), Dominica (➤ 85) and the British Virgin Islands (➤ 80).
Windsurfing: for the best conditions, check out Playa Cabarete, Dominican Republic (➤ 40) and Silver Sands, Barbados (➤ 58).

Horse-riding is a great way to get off the beaten track and explore

Eastern Caribbean

The alluring chain of Eastern Caribbean islands, or Lesser Antilles, curves around from the Virgin Islands to Trinidad, and includes the Dutch ABCs (Aruba, Bonaire and Curaçao) off the coast of Venezuela. Colonised by the British, the French, the Dutch and the Danes, these islands were at the forefront of the 17th- and 18th-century sugar trade, frequently changing hands as the European powers battled for a share of the profits.

Today, the islands can be placed into six groups, plus Barbados, roughly reflecting their colonial history. Working down the chain from the Virgin Islands, the Leeward Islands are interspersed with three of the six Netherlands Antilles and the smaller French Antilles. The larger French islands of Guadeloupe and Martinique fit into the stately volcanic chain of the Windward Islands, and Trinidad and Tobago form a twosome at the tail end.

'I was altogether unprepared for their beauty and grandeur...repeated again and again with every possible variation of the same type of delicate loveliness.'

CHARLES KINGSLEY
At Last, A Christmas in the West Indies
(1871)

●

Echoes of the past: Dutch colonial-style gables on modern Aruba

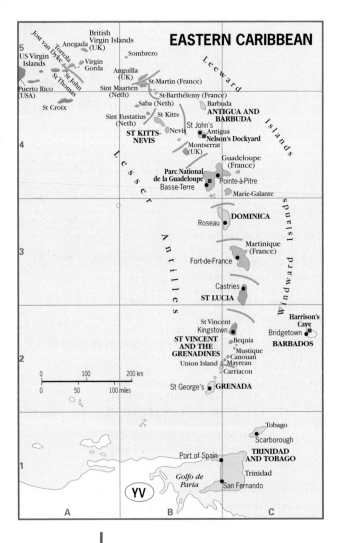

EASTERN CARIBBEAN

Jost van Dyke
Tortola
Anegada
Virgin Gorda
British Virgin Islands (UK)
US Virgin Islands
St John
St Thomas
Puerto Rico (USA)
St Croix
Sombrero
Anguilla (UK)
St-Martin (France)
Sint Maarten (Neth)
St-Barthélemy (France)
Saba (Neth)
Sint Eustatius (Neth)
St Kitts
Nevis
ST KITTS-NEVIS
Barbuda
ANTIGUA AND BARBUDA
St John's
Antigua
Nelson's Dockyard
Montserrat (UK)
Guadeloupe (France)
Parc National de la Guadeloupe
Basse-Terre
Pointe-à-Pitre
Marie-Galante

Leeward Islands

Lesser Antilles

Roseau
DOMINICA
Martinique (France)
Fort-de-France
Castries
ST LUCIA

Windward Islands

St Vincent
Kingstown
ST VINCENT AND THE GRENADINES
Bequia
Mustique
Canouan
Union Island
Mayreau
Carriacou
St George's
GRENADA
Harrison's Cave
Bridgetown
BARBADOS

0		100		200 km

0	50	100 miles

Tobago
Scarborough
TRINIDAD AND TOBAGO
Port of Spain
Golfo de Paria
Trinidad
San Fernando
YV

A   B   C

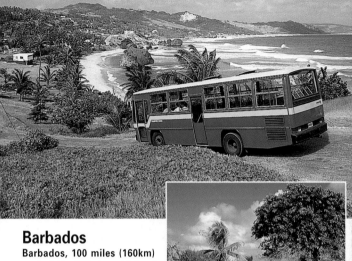

Barbados

Barbados, 100 miles (160km) east of the Windward Island chain, was ruled by the British for three uninterrupted centuries. Today, the colonial legacy of cane fields and plantation houses, incongruously familiar place-names and a passion for cricket lives alongside the Bajans' (Barbadians') own distinctly relaxed and friendly lifestyle. Surrounded by the Atlantic Ocean, the pear-shaped island boasts the famous beaches and exclusive resorts of the Platinum Coast on the sheltered west coast, while the excellent south coast beaches feature more budget-orientated resorts renowned for their lively atmosphere and nightlife. The rocky, wave-lashed east coast of the island is less developed, and inland Barbados is quiet and rural, with pockets of mahogany forest and open grazing land rising to the hilly Scotland district in the northeast.

Atlantic breakers roll ashore at Bathsheba (top), where visitors come to admire the Andromeda Gardens (above)

➕ 54C2
ℹ️ Barbados Tourism Authority, PO Box 242, Harbour Road, Bridgetown ☎ (246) 427-2623; web: www.barbados.org
❓ Crop Over Festival (Jul–Aug)

What to See in Barbados

ANDROMEDA GARDENS ✪✪✪

These glorious botanical gardens, founded in 1954 and represent one of the finest collections of indigenous and exotic tropical trees and plants in the Caribbean. Winding paths crisscross the steep hillside site, with glimpses of the ocean below, climbing through orchid gardens and heliconia and hibiscus areas to shady corners irrigated by tiny streams and waterfalls.

✉️ Bathsheba, St Joseph (on the northeast coast)
☎ (246) 433-9261
🕐 Daily 9–5
♿ Moderate

55

Farley Hill, St Peter
☎ (246) 422-8826
🕐 Daily 10–5
▮ Moderate

 Southwest coast
🍴 Wide selection of cafés and restaurants (£–£££)
ℹ Tourist information kiosk at Bridgetown Harbour cruise-ship terminal

Mount Gay Rum Visitors Centre
✉ Spring Garden Highway
☎ (246) 425-9066
🕐 Mon–Fri 9–4 (tours every 30 minutes)
▮ Moderate

Above: *the Barbados Parliament building in central Bridgetown*

✉ St John
☎ (246) 433-1274
🕐 Daily 10–4

BARBADOS WILDLIFE RESERVE, GRENADE HALL SIGNAL STATION AND FOREST ⭐⭐

Vervet monkeys, Brocket deer, otters, porcupines and iguanas are among the many and varied inhabitants of the 4-acre (1.6ha) mahogany forest reserve, and they are free to wander wherever they choose. For safety's sake the python remains behind bars, and the alligator-like caimans are confined to their pool, but otherwise there is real wildlife spotting to be had while exploring the meandering woodland paths.

Across the car park, the Grenade Hall Signal Station was one of six look-out towers erected in the early 1800s to watch for signs of slave revolts and relay messages from one end of the island to the other using semaphore flags. Nature trails have been laid out through the adjacent Grenade Hall Forest.

BRIDGETOWN ⭐⭐

The energetic island capital, home to around half the 265,000-strong population, radiates from The Careenage, a natural inner harbour where English colonists found an Amerindian bridge in 1625. On the northern waterfront, at the top of the Broad Street shopping district, across from the Parliament Buildings, which date from the 1870s, is National Heroes Square. Near by, St Michael's Cathedral, founded in 1625 but rebuilt on several occasions, records snippets of island history in its numerous inscribed tombstones and tablets.

Bridgetown's busy cruise-ship terminal lies west of the city centre at Bridgetown Harbour. A popular diversion in this area is the **Mount Gay Rum Visitors Centre**, which offers tours. An introduction to the ageing, blending and bottling processes is followed by tastings of the island's most famous rum.

CODRINGTON COLLEGE ⭐

Christopher Codrington, a former Governor of the Leeward Islands and member of one of Barbados's earliest and richest planter families, endowed the 18th-century theological college which now spreads out around his 17th-century childhood home on the southeast coast. The approach, down an avenue of tall and slender palms, is magnificent and the grounds, with water-lily ponds and a forest trail, are open to the public.

FLOWER FOREST ✪

Laid out in the grounds of an old sugar plantation in the rugged Scotland District, the 50-acre (20ha) Flower Forest provides a dazzling introduction to tropical flora. Paths descend through a forest of exotic fruit trees, pink heads of torch ginger, the waxy bracts of heliconias, rustling bamboo and banana plants to a look-out across the hills to the ocean. It's a fair climb back, but there are plenty of interesting stops along the way.

✉ Richmond, St Joseph
☎ (246) 433-8152
🕐 Daily 9–5
💷 Moderate

FRANCIA PLANTATION HOUSE AND GUN HILL SIGNAL STATION ✪✪

Francia is an early 20th-century great house with terraced gardens overlooking the St George Valley, and remains a private home with a working plantation in the rural heart of the island. Guided tours of the elegantly furnished ground floor take in a notable collection of antique prints and one of the earliest maps of the Caribbean region (1522).

Near by, the Gun Hill Signal Station houses a collection of military memorabilia. The stone lion statue on the road below was carved by Captain Henry Wilkinson in 1868.

✉ St George
☎ Francia (246) 429-0474; Gun Hill (246) 429-1358
🕐 Francia, Mon–Fri 10–4; Gun Hill, Mon–Sat 9–5
💷 Cheap

GARRISON SAVANNAH AND THE BARBADOS MUSEUM ✪✪✪

South of Bridgetown, the former British army parade ground of Garrison Savannah has been turned into a racecourse, its grassy track surrounded by imposing 19th-century military buildings and the ruins of two older forts. The entertaining Barbados Museum is housed in the old military prison, an elegant Georgian building flanked by cannons and palm trees. The broad-ranging historical exhibits include a fascinating collection of West Indian maps and engravings dating back to the 1600s.

✉ St Ann's Garrison, St Michael
☎ (246) 427-0201
🕐 Mon–Sat 9–5, Sun 2–6
💷 Moderate

A sweeping stone staircase leads to the door of the Francia plantation house

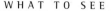

HARRISON'S CAVE (▶ 21, TOP TEN)

HOLETOWN AND THE PORTVALE SUGAR FACTORY AND MUSEUM ✪✪✪

At the heart of the famed Platinum Coast, Holetown was the first settlement on the island, established in 1627. Today, it is home to many of Barbados's smartest hotels.

A few miles inland through the cane fields, Portvale is one of the island's three remaining sugar factories. The best time to visit is during the harvest season (Feb–Jun) when the factory is in full swing, redolent with the treacly smell of molasses. The museum covers the history of the sugar industry accompanied by antique documents, pictures and machinery.

✉ On the west coast

Portvale Sugar Factory and Museum
✉ St James
☎ (246) 432-0100
🕐 Museum, Mon–Sat 9–5; factory, tours Feb–Jun
💷 Museum, cheap; including factory tour, moderate

MORGAN LEWIS SUGAR MILL ✪

The Morgan Lewis mill is the largest surviving windmill in the Caribbean, and was one of the island's 300 sugar-cane grinding mills in the 17th century. A working mill right up until 1944, and a recent addition to the World Monuments Fund's List of 100 Most Endangered Sites in the World, its antique machinery has been restored, and there are grand views across the rolling countryside from the sail loft.

✉ St Andrew
☎ (246) 426-2421
🕐 Daily 9–5
💷 Cheap

A Chattel Village shop in St Lawrence Gap

ST LAWRENCE GAP AND THE SOUTH COAST ✪✪✪

Named after English seaside towns, the south coast resorts of Hastings, Worthing and Dover stretch between Bridgetown and the fishing centre of Oistins, St Lawrence Gap is the liveliest dining and entertainment district on the island and not to be missed. Further east, Silver Sands Beach is a magnet for windsurfing enthusiasts, and there are more secluded sandy coves tucked into the cliffs at Foul Bay, Crane Bay and Long Bay.

✉ Cherry Tree Hill, St Peter
☎ (246) 422-8725
🕐 Mon–Fri 10–3:30
💷 Cheap

ST NICHOLAS ABBEY ✪✪

The Abbey is the oldest historic home on the island of Barbados and a rare example of Jacobean architecture transported to a Caribbean setting. This mid-17th-century great house, with no religious connotations, has a wonderful gabled façade, and guided tours of the antique-filled ground floor reveal all sorts of fascinating details about domestic arrangements in the colonial period. An added bonus is a short home movie depicting Bridgetown and plantation life in 1935.

SUNBURY PLANTATION HOUSE ✪✪

Sunbury, a lovingly restored, 300-year-old great house stuffed full of antique Bajan mahogany furniture, crystal chandeliers, china, silver and comfortably cosy pot plants, was a private home until the 1980s. Now all the rooms are open to view, with four-posters and Victorian frocks displayed upstairs, a carriage museum in the cellar and agricultural machinery in the gardens. Four-course plantation-style dinners are served in the house twice a week (by reservation).

✉ St Philip
☎ (246) 423-6270
🕐 Daily 10–5
💰 Cheap

TYROL COT HERITAGE VILLAGE ✪✪

In the northern suburbs of Bridgetown, 19th-century Tyrol Cot was the family home of Barbados's first post-independence premier, Sir Grantley Adams. The modest, single-storey, coral rock house is furnished with family antiques and memorabilia. In the grounds, the Heritage Village re-creates traditional Bajan chattel houses, simple clapboard cottages built by freed slaves which could be swiftly dismantled and moved, allowing the owner to leave with all his goods and chattels if evicted from a plantation site. Tyrol Cot's chattel houses are used as craft studios and there is a rum shop for refreshments.

✉ Codrington Hill, St Michael
☎ (246) 424-2074
🕐 Mon–Fri 9–5
💰 Cheap

The impressive entrance of St Nicholas Abbey, built around 1650 by Colonel Berringer

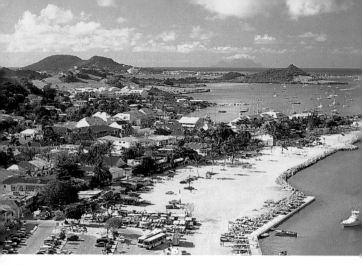

There are fine views of Marigot, the capital of St-Martin, from the hill-fort on the wooded promontory above the bay

The French Antilles

The French Antilles are spread over a distance of 350 miles (560km) from the main islands of Guadeloupe and Martinique in the Windward Island chain to the smaller territories of St Barthélemy and St-Martin, set among the Leeward Island group. The islands' French influence is unmistakable in everything from road signs and croissants to games of *boules* played on shady squares. But the true spirit of the French Antilles is Creole, a zesty French-African enjoyment of life, good food and beautiful women.

What to See in the French Antilles

GUADELOUPE ✪✪

Guadeloupe is actually two islands pushed together by seismic upheaval and linked by a bridge over the Rivière Salée. Grande-Terre, the eastern wing, is a rolling limestone plateau fringed with beaches, and the island's tourist heartland is centred on the south coast. The mountainous western wing, Basse-Terre, contains the towering Soufrière volcano (4,813ft/1,467m), the highest point in the Eastern Caribbean, surrounded by the magnificent rainforest preserve of the Parc National de la Guadeloupe in the south and central region (➤ 24). A tour around the north coast is covered in the Northern Basse-Terre Drive (➤ 62).

Guadeloupe's contrasting halves have equally diverse chief towns. Although the sleepy town of Basse-Terre is the island's administrative capital, the commercial centre of **Pointe-à-Pitre**, in the southwestern corner of Grande-Terre, is far larger and the main entry point for visitors. Guadeloupe's frenetic main port is no Caribbean beauty.

✚ 54B4
ℹ Office Départemental du Tourisme de la Guadeloupe, 5 square de la Banque, 97163 Pointe-à-Pitre ☎ (590) 82-09-30; web: www.francetourism.com
? Carnival (pre-Lent)

Pointe-à-Pitre
✉ Grande-Terre
🍴 Cafés and restaurants (£–£££)
ℹ ➤ above

Behind La Darse, the bustling harbour with its market stalls and ferries departing to the out islands of the Guadeloupean archipelago, the streets are narrow and congested with far too many ugly concrete buildings to be described as picturesque. However, there are pockets of native charm such as the gardens of place de la Victoire, edged by distinctly Gallic cafés and a handful of old colonial houses. A small flower market brightens up the square outside the Cathédral St Pierre et St Paul, and the covered market on rue Frébault is an entertaining collection of stalls piled high with fruit and vegetables, spices and basketware, overseen by voluble matrons.

A short walk west, the **Musée Schoelcher** occupies a pretty French town house. It honours the 19th-century abolitionist Victor Schoelcher, who championed the anti-slavery movement in France, and displays mementoes of the great man together with assorted plantation-era artefacts and paintings.

To the south of town, Bas du Fort's popular marina has several restaurants, and the **Aquarium de la Guadeloupe** (► 109) is the largest in the Caribbean, showcasing strange and exotic tropical fish. Strung along the coast, the busy resort of Gosier and more laidback seaside towns of Ste-Anne and St-François welcome visitors with a wide choice of hotels, restaurants, beaches and watersports. Low-key side-trips include the Pointe des Châteaux, a rocky headland with an orientation table at the eastern tip of the island.

Grande-Terre's only rum producers, **Distillerie Bellevue**, offer tours and rum tastings near Le Moule, Guadeloupe's one-time capital on the east coast, and country roads meander through the unspoilt rural landscape to more beaches in the northwest.

Musée Schoelcher
- 24 rue Peynier
- ☎ (590) 82-08-04
- ⏰ Mon–Fri 8.30–12, 2–5:30; Sat 8:30–12
- 👐 Cheap

Aquarium de la Guadeloupe
- Place Créole-Marina, Bas du Fort
- ☎ (590) 90-92-38
- ⏰ Daily 9–7
- 👐 Moderate

Distillerie Bellevue
- West of Le Moule on the D101 (direction Les Abymes)
- ☎ (590) 23-47-10
- ⏰ Daily 9–5
- 👐 Free

Flower beds provide a splash of winter colour among the trees in Pointe-à-Pitre's place de la Victoire

Northern Basse-Terre

Distance
58 miles/88km

Time
A full day with stops

Start/end point
Pointe-à-Pitre

Lunch
Le Karacoli (£–££)
Grand Anse
☎ (590) 28-41-17

This easy day trip from Pointe-à-Pitre makes a clockwise circuit, crossing the central rainforest highlands before following the northern coast of Basse-Terre.

From Pointe-à-Pitre, cross the Rivière Salée and take the N1 south to the Route de la Traversée (D23).

The cross-island route cuts through the cane fields before beginning the climb into the mountains and the Parc National de la Guadeloupe (➤ 24). Just inside the park boundary, the Cascade aux Ecrevisse is a popular waterfall picnic spot. Further uphill, several rainforest walks and hikes begin from the Maison de la Fôret. From the mountain pass at Col des Mamelles (1,922ft/585m), La Traversée begins the descent to the coast at Mahaut. A short detour south of Mahaut (3 miles/5km), glass-bottomed boat trips to the Cousteau marine reserve at Ilet de Pigeon depart from Plage de Malendure.

Head north from Mahaut along the N2.

Two small local-interest museums are worth a brief stop en route to Pointe Noire. The Maison du Cacao and Maison du Bois tackle the history and applications of cocoa and woodcraft respectively, then continue on to La Grande Anse, which makes a good lunch break and beach opportunity.

Follow the N2 around the northern tip of the island. At Ste-Rose, follow signs to the Musée du Rhum at Bellevue.

The Distillerie Reimonencq offers a chance to sample Guadeloupean rum. Tastings begin with a short film about rum processing, followed by a look around the rum museum, which has added an Insect Gallery to its charms.

Take a break for lunch and a swim at the sandy beach of La Grande Anse, just north of Deshaies

Return to Pointe-à-Pitre on the N2 via Lamentin.

MARTINIQUE ✪✪✪

Martinique, the Carib Indians' *Madinina* (Island of Flowers), is still renowned for its flora as well as for its fine beaches and beautiful women. To the north of the leeward coast capital, Fort-de-France, northern Martinique rises through the lush, green *mornes* (foothills) to the peak of Mont Pelée (4,583ft/1,397m). The southern portion of the island is a rippling carpet of cane fields ringed by beaches, with the main tourist centres dotted along the sheltered west and southern shores.

Martinique's vibrant waterfront capital **Fort-de-France** spreads back into the encircling hills. The harbour is guarded by Fort St-Louis, close to the dock where ferries (*vedettes*) make regular departures for the bayside beaches of Pointe du Bout, Anse Mitan and Anse-à-l'Ane. Behind the waterfront, the La Savane gardens are overlooked by the **Musée Départemental**, which contains notable collections of Amerindian artefacts, and the splendidly bizarre Bibliothèque Schoelcher, designed for the 1889 Paris Exhibition. The main shopping district extends to the north around Cathédral St-Louis.

➕ 54C3

ℹ️ Office Départemental du Tourisme de la Martinique, 2 rue Ernest Deproge, BP 520, 97206 Fort-de-France ☎ (596) 63-79-60; web: www.martinique.org

❓ Carnival (pre-Lent)

Fort-de-France
✉️ West coast
🍴 Plenty of cafés and restaurants (£–£££)

Musée Départemental
✉️ 9 rue de la Liberté
☎ (596) 71-57-05
🕐 Mon–Fri 9–1, 2–5; Sat 9–12
💷 Cheap

The striking art nouveau Bibliothèque Schoelcher was shipped out to Martinique in sections and reassembled

63

Red ginger blooms are among hundreds of exotic tropical spices on show at the Jardin de Balata

Jardin de Balata
- Route de Balata
- (596) 64-48-73
- Daily 9–5
- Cheap

Musée Vulcanologique
- rue Victor Hugo
- (596) 78-15-16
- Daily 9–5
- Cheap

Château Dubuc
- Caravelle Peninsula
- (596) 68-33-06
- Daily 8:30–5:30
- Cheap

Musée de la Pagerie
- Trois-Ilets
- (596) 73-19-30
- Tue–Fri 9–5:30, Sat–Sun 9–1, 2:30–5:30
- Cheap

Ecomusée de Martinique
- Anse Figuiers
- (596) 62-79-14
- Tue–Sun 9–1:30, 2:30–5
- Cheap

Habitation Clément
- D18 south of Le François (direction Le St Esprit)
- (596) 54-62-07
- Daily 9–6
- Moderate

One of the prettiest drives in the Caribbean strikes north out of Fort-de-France on the Route de la Trace (N3) up into the rainforest. Stop off at the gorgeous **Jardin de Balata**, a tropical garden perched high above the coast, before passing beneath the 3,000ft-tall (915m) Pitons du Carbet on a rainforest route lined with steep banks of ferns, bamboo and bromeliad-encrusted trees.

Dropping down to the west coast, St Pierre was once the elegant commercial centre of the island before it was decimated by the eruption of Mont Pelée in 1902. The ruins can be explored and the **Musée Vulcanologique** displays before and after photographs and curios salvaged from the aftermath.

Over on the east coast, there are museums of rum and bananas just north of Ste-Marie, and the attractively wooded Caravelle Peninsula is guarded by the ruins of 17th-century **Château Dubuc**.

South across the bay from Fort-de-France, Pointe du Bout and the beach at Anse Mitan are the island's busiest resort areas, close to the pretty fishing village of Trois-Ilets, where Napoléon Bonaparte's wife, Empress Joséphine, was born. The **Musée de la Pagerie**, in a simple stone cottage, displays mementoes of the empress's Caribbean childhood and letters from the future French emperor.

Due south, the coastal road reaches a clifftop look-out with views of Rocher du Diamant, a rocky offshore outcrop once occupied by a British naval garrison intent on harrying French shipping. East of Ste-Luce, across the Rivière Pilote, the **Ecomusée de Martinique** provides a fascinating French-language account of local history, augmented by models and Amerindian and colonial relics.

The breezy yachting centre of Le Marin lies just north of Ste-Anne, a charming small seaside town and resort close to the fabulous sun-baked sands of Grande Anse des Salines, which stretch down to the southern tip of the island.

Sidewalk tables outside a local restaurant in Marigot, the capital of French St-Martin

The **Habitation Clément** sugar estate, at St-François on the east coast, opens its *chais* (storehouses) for inspection, packed from floor to ceiling with barrels of maturing vintage rum. There are tastings, and a charming antique-filled, 19th-century plantation house to visit.

ST-BARTHÉLEMY ✪✪
Super-chic St-Barthélemy is probably the most expensive and exclusive outpost in the Caribbean though it covers just 8sq miles (20sq km). Indisputably French from its *haute couture* boutiques to its baguettes, St-Barts is a magnet for the rich and famous. Shopping and people-watching are the chief pastimes in the island's picturesque port capital, Gustavia, named in honour of King Gustav III during a century of Swedish rule (1785–1878). There is also a pleasant stroll around the harbour to the **Musée de Saint-Barth** and its local history and crafts exhibits.

Beyond Gustavia, the resort village of St-Jean faces a fine bay beach with watersports. On the south coast, Anse de Grande Saline and Anse du Gouverneur offer dazzling stretches of undeveloped sandy shore.

ST-MARTIN ✪✪
The French half of Sint Maarten/St-Martin is a relaxing antidote to its over-developed and over-visited Dutch counterpart (► 77). Only the West Indian stallholders in the waterfront market give any hint that Marigot, the capital, is a Caribbean town, not a corner of mainland France. Boulevard de France and Marina Port La Royale are the twin poles of café society, and there are fine views over the town from the hilltop ruins of 18th-century Fort St-Louis. St-Martin arguably boasts the best beaches on the island, with Baie Longue, Baie Rouge and Baie Nettlé in the west, and Baie Orientale, on the east coast. Grand Case is another beach resort, famous for its Restaurant Row, with many of the island's finest restaurants.

➕ 54B4
🍴 Good selection of cafés and restaurants (£–£££)
ℹ️ Office du Tourisme, quai du Général de Gaulle, 97133 Gustavia
☎ (590) 27-87-27

Musée de Saint-Barth
✉️ rue Alvar
☎ (590) 27-89-07
🕐 Mon–Thu 8:30–12:30, 2:30–6; Fri 8:30–12:30, 3–6; Sat 8:30–11
✋ Cheap

➕ 54B5
🍴 Wide choice of cafés and restaurants (£–£££)
ℹ️ Office du Tourisme, boulevard de France, 97150 Marigot ☎ (590) 87-57-21; web: www.interknowledge.com/st-martin
❓ Carnival (pre-Lent)

Food & Drink

Caribbean cooking is generally simple and unpretentious. Staple foods such as rice 'n' peas (the 'peas' are red kidney beans), spinach-like callaloo soup, fresh fish and a wide variety of fruit and vegetables – plantains, christophene (a tropical marrow) and breadfruit – are found throughout the region.

However, culinary traditions vary from island to island and the combination of influences – African, British, French, Dutch, East Indian, Spanish and South American – produces plenty of variation from hearty platters of spicy Jamaican jerk (meat and fish cooked in barbecue pits) to the more refined gourmet dishes of French Creole cuisine.

Island specialities

The French islands of Guadeloupe and Martinique take good food very seriously. Favourite Creole specialities include *blaff* (fish or shellfish stew cooked in a wine and herb court-bouillon), *crabes farcis* (stuffed land crabs) and *accras* (battered fish balls). *Lambi* (conch tenderised with lime) is a popular ingredient in salads, fritters and chowders, and most menus feature a choice of traditional *colombos* (meat and chicken curries).

Spicy Jamaican jerk pork (above) and fresh Caribbean lobster (below) are popular local specialities

Adventurous gourmets will find another traditionally French culinary speciality served in Dominica, where 'mountain chicken' (frogs' legs) is considered a local delicacy. A common Windward Island staple is pepperpot, a spicy meat stew accompanied by lashings of hot sauce. Bottles of incendiary red or sometimes yellow (coloured with tumeric) pepper sauce adorn every local restaurant table and their contents should be treated with caution.

Trinidad is justly famous for its eclectic national cuisine which has been heavily influenced by East Indian and Chinese migrants. Generous Indian-style snacks, such as *roti* (chapati envelopes filled with curried meat, fish or vegetables) and *doubles* (with a spiced chickpea filling), are favourite items in the local fast-food pantheon. Snacking in Puerto Rico is also highly recommended. Abandon the American fast-food chains and bland international hotel cuisine for tasty Spanish-influenced *alcapurrias* (savoury or sweet fritters), *empanadas* (meat- or vegetable-filled pastry pockets) and tasty *picadillos* (the local variation on a beefburger). Classic main dishes include *arroz con pollo* (chicken and rice cooked in coconut milk).

In the Dutch islands, one of the chief ingredients of *keshi yena* is Gouda cheese mixed with chicken, fish or savoury minced beef and raisins, while all the Indonesian restaurants bear witness to Dutch colonial involvement in southeast Asia.

A traditional dish of saltfish and ackee (a fleshy yellow tree vegetable that looks like scrambled egg)

Drinks

Whether it be dark, light, spiced, fruit-flavoured or mixed into creamy liqueur-type concoctions, rum is the favourite tipple throughout the Caribbean. Traditionally, the best rums come from Barbados, Jamaica, Guadeloupe and Martinique. Puerto Rico (Bacardi) and St Croix (Cruzan) are renowned for white rums, and many islands produce a local brew. The Caribbean cocktail hour, long on punches, piña coladas and exotic daiquiris, is a homage to the versatility of rum.

An old recipe for rum punch: one sour (lemon), two sweet (sugar), three strong (rum) and four weak (water)

Locally brewed beers are also recommended – and are much cheaper than imported brands. Look out for Banks in Barbados, Piton in St Lucia, Presidente in the Dominican Republic, Hairoun from St Vincent, and Carib, Jamaica's Red Stripe.

Thirst-quenching fruit juices come in a selection of delicious flavours, from mango and pineapple to the more unusual – but utterly delectable – soursop, tamarind and sugar apple.

The Leeward Islands

Stopping the gap between the Virgin Islands and the Windward Island chain are the British Crown Colonies of Anguilla and Montserrat, and the independent English-speaking twin-island countries of Antigua and Barbuda, and St Kitts and Nevis, which form the Leeward Island group. Lively Antigua is the most developed holiday destination in the Leewards, while Anguilla has a selection of the finest beaches and most luxurious hotels in the Caribbean. St Kitts and Nevis are renowned for their laidback lifestyle and gracious plantation-style hotels. Volcanic Montserrat is currently a no-go area for tourists due to recent eruptions.

What to See in the Leeward Islands

ANGUILLA ✪✪

A low-lying, coral limestone strand at the northern tip of the Leewards, Anguilla incorporates some 30 stunning beaches and sandy coves that compare favourably with the best in the world. The shallow, turquoise sea is a snorkeller's delight and source of the delicious spiny lobsters for which the island is famous, and the diving here is superb (► 112).

The Valley is Anguilla's diminutive capital, where the pint-sized **Anguilla National Museum** doubles as the headquarters of the Anguilla National Trust. The Trust can arrange natural history, birdwatching and turtle walks and visits to Amerindian sites, but the real focus of the island is the shore. Anguilla's liveliest beach is Shoal Bay on the north coast, 1½ miles (2.5km) of dazzling white ankle-deep sand with watersports concessions. Near the East End, Captain's Bay and Savannah Bay are both secluded and undeveloped, while the 2-mile (3km) south coast strip of Rendezvous Bay is another beauty facing St-Martin.

✚ 54B5
ℹ Anguilla Tourist Board, PO Box 1388, The Valley, Anguilla, just outside Wallblake Airport ☎ (264) 497-2759; web: www.candw.com.ai/~atb tour

❓ Carnival (Aug)

Anguilla National Museum
✉ The Valley
☎ (264) 497-5297
🕐 Mon–Fri 8–4
💵 Donations

A local lobster fisherman displays his catch on the shores of Anguilla's turquoise Maunday's Bay

ANTIGUA ✪✪✪

Like Anguilla, and its sister island of Barbuda to the north, Antigua (pronounced *An-teega*) is a dry limestone coral island ringed by gorgeous white sand beaches. It is the largest of the Leewards at 108sq miles (280sq km), an important regional transport hub and major yachting centre. The high point of the sailing calendar is Antigua Race Week at the end of the December to April yachting season, which draws an impressive field of international competitors for the week-long series of races, regattas and serious partying.

Columbus sighted Antigua in 1493, and named it Santa Maria de la Antigua after a miraculous statue of the Virgin Mary in Seville Cathedral. With the exception of brief incursions by the Spanish and French in the early days, Britain held the island from 1632 until independence in 1981. Sugar-cane was introduced in the 1670s, and settlers planted the island from end to end decimating the natural vegetation. Today, shorn of its cane carpet, Antigua's interior is generally arid and scrubby, still dotted with the ruins of old stone sugar mills. During the 18th and 19th centuries, the British navy made full use of the strategically important safe anchorages at Falmouth and English Harbour. Lord Nelson once served an uncomfortable posting at English Harbour, where the restored Georgian navy base renamed in his honour is the focus of the fascinating Nelson's Dockyard National Park (► 22).

🔂 54B4

ℹ️ Antigua and Barbuda Division of Tourism, Nevis Street and Friendly Alley, St John's, Antigua
☎ (268) 462-0480; web: www.interknowledge.com/antigua-barbuda

🎭 Carnival (Jul–Aug)

Above: a hilltop view from Shirley Heights across English Harbour to Nelson's Dockyard and Falmouth

DID YOU KNOW?

When Nelson sailed for England in 1787, he ordered a barrel of rum to be taken on board to preserve his body for a home burial if he died on the six-week voyage.

Above: *cruise passengers disembark in St John's*
Right: *traditional wood and stone built town houses*

St John's

✉ West coast

🍴 Good selection of cafés and restaurants (£–£££)

ℹ See panel ➤ 69

Museum of Antigua and Barbuda

✉ Corner of Long and Market Streets

☎ (268) 462-4930

🕐 Mon–Fri 8:30–4, Sat 10–2

💰 Donations

St John's, Antigua's busy capital and cruise port, is well worth a visit. A tight grid of narrow streets and alleys first laid out in 1702 climbs gently uphill from the bustling waterfront district towards the silver topped towers of St John's Cathedral. Cruise passengers come ashore by the Heritage Quay duty-free complex right in the heart of downtown. One block over, Redcliffe Quay is lined with attractively restored old wooden buildings offering a more interesting selection of shops. A short walk up Long Street, the **Museum of Antigua and Barbuda** makes an interesting introduction to local history and culture. Assorted exhibits range from pre-Columbian artefacts left by the islands' original Siboney and Arawak inhabitants to Viv Richards' cricket bat. The former captain of both the Antiguan and West Indian cricket teams is a national hero.

Three miles (5km) north of the capital, Dickenson Bay is Antigua's premier tourist beach and a lively spot without being overdeveloped. Its modest clutch of low-rise resort hotels line the broad half-mile-long (1km) stretch of fine white sand offering a choice of restaurants and beach bars, and watersports concessions hire out windsurfers and sail boats.

In the centre of the island, the **Betty's Hope** plantation was established in the 1650s and grew into one of Antigua's chief sugar producers. Although the cane fields have long since disappeared, one of the original windmills has been restored to working order, while a small museum explores the history of the sugar industry and plantation life.

Way out on the east coast of the island, **Devil's Bridge** was hollowed out of the limestone cliffs by crashing Atlantic surf. This natural arch is a popular tourist site on round-island tours, particularly on a blustery day when waves forced up through holes in the rock create giant waterspouts.

Antigua's top sightseeing attraction is the Nelson's Dockyard National Park (▶ 22) on the south coast. High above English Harbour, the ruins of the Shirley Heights garrison command superb views over the dockyard, down the island and off to neighbouring Guadeloupe. The former guard house now houses the Shirley Heights Lookout, which hosts a famous Sunday afternoon barbecue and reggae jump-up.

Between All Saints and Liberta (one of the first villages founded by freed slaves) in the central south region of the island, look for the **Fig Tree Drive** turn-off. The prettiest drive on Antigua, this quiet back road meanders down to the coast through a rare pocket of natural vegetation which escaped the sugar boom clearances of the 17th and 18th centuries. There are lovely views down to the sea, and banana plants ('figs' in local parlance), wild mango, guava and palm trees line the roadside, with the hills to the west rising up to Boggy Peak (1,319ft/402m), the highest point on the island.

West along the shore, the dazzling crescent of pale sand and azure sea at Dark Wood Beach makes an irresistible beach break though its elegant fringe of palm trees was sadly truncated by Hurricane Luis in 1995. Visit on a weekday, when it is virtually deserted; things hot up considerably on the weekend.

The military abandoned Shirley Heights in 1850, but many of the garrison's coral stone ruins survive

Betty's Hope
- ✉ Southeast of Pares
- ☎ (268) 462-1469
- 🕐 Tue–Sat 10–4
- 🎫 Free

Devil's Bridge
- ✉ 1½ miles (2km) east of Indian Town, east coast

Fig Tree Drive
- ✉ St Mary's Parish, between Swetes and Old Road

St Kitts

This circuit around northern St Kitts makes a leisurely day trip incorporating historic sites, marvellous views and a lunch stop at one of the island's finest plantation hotels.

From Basseterre, take the coast road west past Bloody Point, where European settlers defeated the Caribs, to Old Road Town.

A quiet fishing village, Old Road Town was the original capital of St Kitts. A side-road leads past a large boulder adorned with Amerindian carvings to Romney Manor. The 17th-century manor now houses the Caribelle Batik textile workshops (➤ 106). Visitors are welcome and there is an on-site shop.

With views to the coast, the veranda at the Rawlins Plantation is perfectly placed to catch the breeze

Distance
30 miles (48km)

Time
A day trip with stops

Start/end point
Basseterre

Lunch
Rawlins Plantation (££)
✉ St Paul's
☎ (869) 465-6221

Continue north along the shore to Brimstone Hill.

The Brimstone Hill Fortress crowns a rocky outcrop with splendid views off to the neighbouring islands of Sint Eustatius (in the foreground) and Saba. Nicknamed the 'Gibraltar of the West Indies', the colossal fort was founded by the British in 1690. A small museum displays finds including Amerindian artefacts, old clay pipes and musket balls.

From Brimstone, the road circles around the north of the island through the cane fields to St Paul's. Just beyond the village is a right turn on to the bumpy track to the Rawlins Plantation.

Set in the grounds of this lovely plantation inn, the Plantation Picture House is the studio of well-known local artist Kate Spencer.

Continue on the main road through Sadlers to Black Rocks.

This jagged spur of wave-lashed black volcanic rocks was formed by ancient lava flows from Mount Liamuiga.

The round–island road travels back down the east coast for Basseterre.

ST KITTS

Carib Indians named it *Liamuiga* (Fertile Land); Columbus plumped for St Christopher, his namesake and the patron saint of travellers; and the English shortened it to St Kitts after establishing their first successful Caribbean colony here in 1623. St Kitts is shaped rather like a tadpole, with a round-island road circling the lush rainforest heights of Mount Liamuiga (3,793ft/1,156m) in the north (➤ opposite). The island's arid tail, which sports the best beaches, trails off down to The Narrows, a 2-mile-wide (3km) channel that separates St Kitts from its tiny twin sister, Nevis (➤ 23).

The island capital Basseterre ('low ground' in French) dates from the days when French as well as English colonists laid claim to the island. Behind the new waterfront cruise-ship development, the compact old town centre radiates from The Circus and its Victorian clock tower which serves as a local landmark and meeting place. The neighbouring streets of two-storeyed Georgian wood and stone buildings with gingerbread trimmings contain a small but entertaining selection of shops, galleries and courtyard restaurants.

At the head of the peninsula, south of Basseterre, Frigate Bay is St Kitts' main resort area with a sheltered sandy beach on the west coast and rougher waves on the eastern shore. There is a quieter beach retreat at lovely South Friar's Bay, and a 10-mile (16km) roller-coaster road swings down to The Narrows and a clutch of small beaches facing Nevis. Turtle Beach is a favourite with a lively beach bar and watersports.

54B4

St Kitts and Nevis Department of Tourism, Pelican Mall, Bay Road, Basseterre, St Kitts
☎ (869) 465-4040; web: www.interknowledge.com/stkitts-nevis

National Carnival (Dec–Jan), Music Festival (Jul)

Traditional skirt-and-blouse (wood above stone) architecture surrounding The Circus clock tower

The city of Oranjestad spreads off to the horizon behinds its downtown heart and busy cruise port

Netherlands Antilles

Three and a half centuries of Dutch rule have left a firm imprint on the Netherlands Antilles, a total of four and a half islands, plus Aruba, which was granted autonomy in 1986. Geographically, they are divided into two groups with the ABC Islands (Aruba, Bonaire, Curaçao) off the coast of South America; and the SSS Islands (Saba, Sint Eustatius, and the Dutch half of Sint Maarten/St-Martin) 500 miles (800km) to the north.

What to See in the Netherlands Antilles

ARUBA ⭐⭐

It is thought Aruba was first sighted by Alonso de Ojeda in 1499, and claimed for Spain. However, early colonists declared it an *isla inútil* (useless island), and the arid, scrubby island was not settled for more than a century. Aruba's early 20th-century prosperity was founded on oil, but since the 1980s the island has capitalised on its dry climate and fabulous beaches which are well developed for tourism.

Oranjestad, Aruba's capital, is a popular cruise-ship destination. Behind the waterfront shopping malls and Nassaustraat shopping district, the old town offers Dutch Colonial-style buildings on Wilhelminastraat, and a local history museum housed in **Fort Zoutman**, the island's oldest building, which has guarded the harbour since its completion in 1796.

North of the city, the island's two finest beaches and resort areas, Palm Beach and Eagle Beach, are nicknamed

🔶 29D2

ℹ️ Aruba Tourism Authority, L.G. Smith Boulevard 172, Oranjestad ☎ (297) 823777

🎭 Carnival (pre-Lent)

Oranjestad

✉️ South coast

🍴 Wide range of dining options (£–£££)

Fort Zoutman Historical Museum

✉️ Off L.G. Smith Boulevard

☎️ (297) 826099

🕐 Mon–Fri 10–12, 1:30–4:30

 Cheap

the 'high-rise strip' and the 'low-rise strip' respectively. A wide variety of watersports are on offer here, and there are plenty of bars and restaurants to choose from.

A tour of Aruba's natural landmarks might start with Natural Bridge, a 100ft-long (30m) span of coral rock hollowed out by wave action on the north coast. Visitors can scale the modest heights of the Hooiberg, a 541ft (165m) mini-mountain in the centre of the island. There are also several excellent small beaches around the southernmost tip of the island.

BONAIRE ✪

Smallest and least developed of the ABCs, Bonaire is a mecca for divers who come to experience the superb Bonaire Marine Park (➤ 17).

The pint-sized capital of Kralendijk lies in the sheltered curve of the west coast, close to the best dive sites. A circular drive leads south past the rosy sands of Pink Beach and the salt works on the shallow Pekelmeer lagoon, home to one of Bonaire's famous flamingo colonies, to a row of abandoned slave huts on the shore. In the north, the Washington-Slagbaai National Park is criss-crossed by marked walking and driving trails allowing a close-up look at hardy native flora, Mount Brandaris (787ft/240m), Bonaire's highest point, and the Goto Meer flamingo breeding ground.

🟥 29D2
ℹ️ Bonaire Tourist Office, Kaya Libertador Simon Bolivar 12, Kralendijk
☎ (5997) 8322
❓ Carnival (pre-Lent)

CURAÇAO ✪✪

Curaçao's pride and joy is the historic capital of Willemstad, one of the most picturesque cities in the Caribbean. The old town's heart and main shopping district is the Punda, fronted by an eye-catching collection of gabled Dutch colonial buildings, and Fort Amsterdam on the Handelskade waterfront. Willemstad's floating market is a popular sight around the corner on Waaigat, and the **Mikveh Israel-Emmanuel Synagogue** is the oldest synagogue in the Americas, founded in 1732.

Curaçao's main resort areas are on the west coast either side of Willemstad. To the south, Seaquarium Beach is one of the island's liveliest, with a showcase for local marine life at the Curaçao Seaquarium, as well as good snorkelling and diving (➤ 112).

Land-based diversions include hiking in the northern Christoffel National Park and touring the dry and rugged cunucu backcountry on the look-out for restored Dutch Colonial *landhuisen* (country houses).

🟥 29D2
ℹ️ Curaçao Tourism Development Bureau, Petermaai 19 (PO Box 3266), Willemstad
☎ (5999) 461-6000
❓ Carnival (pre-Lent)

Mikveh Israel-Emmanuel Synagogue and Jewish Museum
✉️ Hanci di Snoa
☎ (5999) 461-1633
🕐 Mon–Fri 9–11:45, 2:30–5
💲 Cheap

Above: *Willemstad's Handelskade waterfront, Curaçao*

54B4

Saba Tourist Bureau,
Windwardside ☎ (5994)
62231

Carnival (Jul–Aug)

Saba Museum
✉ Windwardside
🕓 Mon–Fri 10–12, 1–3:30
💰 Cheap

Above: *Windwardside's
whitewashed, red-roofed
cottages cling to the
hillside in the highlands
of Saba*

54B4

Sint Eustatius Tourism
Development Foundation,
Oranjestad ☎ (5993)
82433

Carnival (Jul)

**Sint Eustatius Historical
Foundation Museum**
✉ Simon Doncker House,
Wilhelminaweg,
Oranjestad
🕓 Mon–Fri 9–5, Sat 9–12
💰 Cheap

SABA ✪✪

Saba is the smallest of the Netherlands Antilles, a rugged volcanic peak rising almost sheer from the sea 30 miles (48km) south of Sint Maarten. The island is quiet and rural, dominated by the towering green bulk of Mount Scenery (2,885ft/879m), with four small villages of whitewashed, red-roofed houses clinging to the foothills. Saba's chief draw is the Saba Marine Park (▶ 112–13), and its fans rave about the blissfully relaxed pace of life.

The Bottom is Saba's minuscule capital, but most visitors head for the village of Windwardside nestled 2,000ft (610m) up in the mountains. Here, among cottage gardens ablaze with hibiscus and bougainvillea, and craft shops selling Saban lace, the Saba Museum juxtaposes Amerindian relics with colonial antiques. Windwardside is also a good start point for treks up Mount Scenery, following a 1,064-step trail through the rainforest.

SINT EUSTATIUS ✪

Tiny Sint Eustatius was once a thriving 18th-century trading post, so wealthy it was known as Golden Rock, and its waterfront warehouses were piled high with silver, guns, sugar and silk. These days, Statia (pronounced *Stay-sha*) is a sleepy backwater with a handful of simple hotels catering to divers and hikers.

The main settlement of Oranjestad is divided into two levels by a 100ft (30m) cliff. On the upper level, traditional wooden buildings gather in the lee of 17th-century Fort Oranje, and the Sint Eustatius Historical Foundation Museum displays Arawak Indian and colonial artefacts in a restored 18th-century brick house.

The best of Statia's dozen or so walking trails scale The Quill to the crater rim of Mount Mazinga, 2,000ft (610m) above sea-level. Inside the crater bowl there is a luxuriant rainforest jungle and locals come here at night to hunt land crabs, a Statian culinary treat.

SINT MAARTEN ✪✪✪

Sint Maarten/St-Martin (▶ 65) is the smallest island (37sq miles/95sq km) in the world to be divided between two sovereign states. The Dutch–French division dates back to 1648, and although France gained the lion's share, relations are amicable and the island is one of the most prosperous and developed enclaves in the Caribbean.

The Dutch capital, Philipsburg, is the main entry point to the island, a top cruise-ship destination and second only to St Thomas in the duty-free shopping stakes. The main action takes place on Front Street, a teeming mile-long shopper's paradise.

Sint Maarten's best beaches stretch along the coast northwest of town. The road leads out past Cole Bay and Simpson Bay to the tourists' favourite, Mullet Bay, with a wide range of watersports, shops and a golf course.

Right: *local wall art*
Below: *beach restaurant with a view, Philipsburg*

☩ 54B5
🛈 Sint Maarten Tourist Office, W Nisbeth Road 23, Philipsburg ☎ (5995) 22337; web: www.st-maarten.com. Information kiosk by the Philipsburg cruise-ship pier on Wathey Square
❓ Carnival (pre-Lent)

A Trinidadian craftswoman models one of her bestselling woven palm-leaf creations

Trinidad & Tobago

Trinidad and Tobago, the twin-island nation at the southern tip of the Caribbean island chain, make an odd couple. Loud, boisterous, multicultural Trinidad is home to the cosmopolitan capital, Port of Spain, and the famous Carnival. A relative newcomer in the tourism stakes, Trinidad is a naturalist's paradise with many birds and butterflies and a range of plant life unrivalled in the region. Laidback, rural Tobago has an untamed rainforest heart, terrific diving and a low-key tourist industry centred on a few south coast beaches.

What to See in Trinidad & Tobago

TRINIDAD ✪

Broken off the South American mainland as recently as 10,000 years ago, Trinidad was claimed for Spain by Columbus in 1498. The island welcomed French planters in the 18th century, before passing to Britain in 1802. After the abolition of slavery, plantation owners hired East Indian indentured labourers, and descendants of these Indians and former African slaves now make up around 40 per cent of the population each.

The teeming streets of Port of Spain reflect Trinidad's complex multicultural heritage. A modern city has sprung up amid a welter of West Indian gingerbread homes, British colonial piles, mosques, markets and the wide open spaces of Queen's Park Savannah. Here a collection of

🚹 54C1
ℹ️ Tourist and Industrial Development Company (TIDCO), 10–14 Philipps Street, Port of Spain
☎ (868) 623-6022; web: www.tidco.co.tt.
Information kiosks at Trinidad's Piarco Airport and Tobago's Crown Point Airport ☎ (868) 639-0509
❓ Trinidad Carnival (pre-Lent), Tobago Heritage Festival (Jul)

Charlottesville, on Tobago's north coast, basks in the evening sunshine

grandiose old mansions has earned the nickname 'The Magnificent Seven', while the Botanical Gardens and Emperor Valley Zoo (► 109) feature a fine array of tropical flora and fauna. On Frederick Street, the **National Museum and Art Gallery** traces island history and culture with an interesting Carnival section. Further down the street, Indian markets and street stalls provide entertaining and lively shopping.

The evening flight of the scarlet ibis at the **Caroni Bird Sanctuary** south of Port of Spain is a fabulous sight. Boat safaris head into the 450-acre (180ha) marshland and mangrove swamp preserve to catch the dazzling show. A wonderful place to study native hummingbirds and other forest species is the **Asa Wright Nature Centre**, high in the hills of the Northern Range east of the capital. Trails and guided walks explore forest paths and there is a swimming-hole for cooling off.

TOBAGO ●●●

Tobago is a typically relaxed and easy-going West Indian island with an attitude and appearance more similar to its Windward Island neighbours than upbeat Trinidad. A handful of beautiful beaches border the south coast, where most visitors stay. Palm-fringed Pigeon Point is a famously picturesque strand with access to snorkelling in the Buccoo Reef National Park, though the best dive sites are found off the north-coast villages of Charlotteville and Speyside (► 112). The upland Tobago Forest Reserve is prime hiking country, and there are short walks to beauty spots such as the Argyle Falls, and King's Bay Falls set back from the east coast.

Scarborough, the appealingly ramshackle capital, is worth a quick visit. Clapboard houses spread uphill from the harbour and market area past a clutch of old colonial buildings, including the 1825 House of Assembly, to 18th-century Fort George. By the fort, the **Tobago Museum** houses a terrific collection of Amerindian finds including pottery and tools.

National Museum and Art Gallery
⊠ 117 Frederick Street, Port of Spain
☎ (868) 623-5941
⊕ Tue–Sat 10–6
⊌ Free

Caroni Bird Sancturay
⊠ Uriah Butler Highway
☎ (868) 645-1305
⊕ Daily
⊌ Moderate charge for boat tours
⁇ Tours for Ibis flight depart around 4:30PM

Asa Wright Nature Centre
⊠ Arima Valley
☎ (868) 667-4655
⊕ Daily 9–5
⊌ Moderate
⁇ Guided walks 10AM and 1:30PM

➕ 54C1
ℹ Unit 12, TIDCO Mall, Sangster's Hill, Scarborough ☎ (868) 639-4333, or at airport (► opposite)

Tobago Museum
⊠ Fort King George
☎ (868) 639-3970
⊕ Mon–Fri 9–5
⊌ Cheap

Top: *the red rooftops of Tortola, with the island of Gunia in the background*
Above: *on the dockside at Soper's Hole Marina in the west end of Tortola*

54A5
Foxy's Beach Bar, Great Harbour (£)
Ferries from West End, Tortola

The Virgin Islands

Scattered across 1,000sq miles (2,589sq km), the 100-plus islands, cays, reefs and rocks of the Virgin Islands archipelago are divided between the magnificently laid-back British Virgin Islands (BVI) and the more developed US Virgin Islands (USVI; ► 82–4).

British Virgin Islands

Low-key and friendly, the rugged green islands of the BVI flank Drake's Passage, a broad sea channel named for Sir Francis Drake who navigated these tricky, pirate-infested waters in 1585. Today, the same hidden coves and secluded bays beloved of 16th-century pirates are a haven for sun-worshippers and yachtspeople exploring one of the world's most desirable yachting destinations.

What to See in the British Virgin Islands

JOST VAN DYKE   ✪

A stone's throw north of Tortola, this tiny island makes a great away-day escape, with beautiful beaches and little in the way of tourist facilities. The island was named for a Dutch pirate who would probably have enjoyed the island's famous New Year's Eve beach party. Some 2,000 revellers descend for the night, then disappear, leaving the islanders to sleep it off until the next year.

Ferries arrive at the grandly named Great Harbour, a sleepy collection of faded West Indian houses on the bay. Another popular beach is White Bay, to the west.

TORTOLA ✪✪

On the north side of Drake's Passage, Tortola is the largest of the BVIs, measuring 11 miles by 3 miles (17km by 5km). The modest capital of Road Town gathers behind the broad bay and ferry terminal with a small selection of craft shops, a pub and an historical museum on Main Street. To the east, the **J R O'Neal Botanic Gardens** make a pleasant detour laid out around a water-lily pond, with an orchid house and wooden benches shaded by palm trees.

The high ridge running down the centre of the island is dominated by Mount Sage (1,780ft/542m). From the **Sage Mountain National Park** there are fabulous views across the BVI, and trails plunge into the primeval rainforest edged by giant ferns and glossy elephant-ear vines.

Tortola's best beaches are on the north coast, where Cane Garden Bay is well equipped with watersports concessions. At the western tip of the island, Soper's Hole is an attractive marina and waterfront shopping complex. Ferries for Jost van Dyke (BVI) and the USVI (St John and St Thomas) depart from the West End dock.

VIRGIN GORDA ✪✪✪

A 5-mile (8km) hop east of Tortola, the 'fat virgin' (so named because Columbus thought it resembled a pregnant woman) was 'rediscovered' by Laurance Rockefeller, who established the first of several low-key but luxurious resorts here in the 1960s. Ferries arrive at The Valley (also called Spanish Town) on the southwest coast. Near by, The Baths are Virgin Gorda's most visited site, a photogenic beachside jumble of massive boulders, caves and grottoes. On the road north, there are quieter beaches at Savannah Bay, fantastic views across Drake's Passage and the stunning yachting centre of North Sound, and hiking trails up Gorda Peak, at 1,358ft (414m), the island's highest point.

🗺 54A5
ℹ BVI Tourist Board, Ferry Terminal (PO Box 134), Road Town, Tortola
☎ (284) 494-3134
🍴 Cafés and restaurants (£–£££)
❓ Festival (Jul–Aug)

J R O'Neal Botanic Gardens
✉ Botanic Road
☎ (284) 494-4557
🕐 Daily 8–6
💵 Donations

Sage Mountain National Park
🕐 Open site
💵 Free

ℹ Tourist Information, Virgin Gorda Yacht Harbour
☎ (284) 495-5181
⛴ Ferries to The Valley from Road Town, Tortola; and North Sound from Beef Island, Tortola

The unique formations of smooth granite boulders known as 'the Baths', on the southwest tip of Virgin Gorda

✚ 54A4

ℹ️ US Virgin Islands
Department of Tourism,
PO Box 640, Charlotte
Amalie, St Thomas, USVI
00804 ☎ (340) 774-
8784; web:
www.usvi.net

US Virgin Islands

**Upbeat and indubitably American St Thomas, and
neighbouring St John, which is for the most part a
national park (► 25), are the two most visited
Virgin Islands. Some 40 miles (65km) due south, St
Croix is quieter, but offers more in the way of
sightseeing.**

The Danish West India Company claimed St Thomas and
St John in the late 17th century, later purchasing St Croix
from the French in 1733. All three were sold to the US for
$25 million in 1917, and are unincorporated territories of
the United States.

What to See in the US Virgin Islands

ℹ️ St Croix Tourist
Information, Queen Cross
Street, Christiansted ☎
(340) 773-0495; web:
www.st-croix.com

🎭 Crucian Christmas
Festival (Dec–6 Jan)

Fort Christiansvaern

✉️ Christiansted National
Historic Site

☎ (340) 773-1460

🕐 Mon–Fri 8–5, Sat–Sun
9–5

💷 Cheap

ST CROIX ⚫⚫

South of the main archipelago, St Croix (pronounced Croy)
is the largest of the Virgin Islands at 82sq miles
(212sq km). This prosperous sugar-growing colony during
the plantation era jockeyed for position with St Thomas
until pretty St Thomas cornered the tourist market in the
1960s. However, St Croix still has plenty to recommend it,
not least the gentle pace and courtesy of its islanders.

The Danish influence is alive and well in the capital of
Christiansted. Laid out in 1733, and named in honour of
King Christian VI, the historic heart of town leads back
from the waterfront in a grid of attractive shopping streets
and arcaded stone buildings dating from the 18th and 19th
centuries. A stroll around the battlements of **Fort
Christiansvaern** is a must. The pristine little yellow-and-
white fort was largely constructed between 1738 and
1749, and bristles with cannons which were never fired in

DID YOU KNOW?

Columbus was so captivated by the beauty of the Virgin Islands he named them after the legend of St Ursula and her retinue of 11,000 beautiful virgins.

A cruise ship dwarfs the yachts at anchor off Charlotte Amalie, the capital of the USVI

anger. Another small but fascinating stop is the **St Croix Aquarium**, showcasing all sorts of strange and frequently beautiful creatures found in local waters. Many of them can be spotted around **Buck Island** Reef National Monument, an 850-acre (344ha) offshore island claiming St Croix's best beach and excellent coral reef snorkelling reached by boat rides (one hour) from Christiansted (daily trips 9AM and 1PM).

A 30-minute drive from the capital down Centerline Road to the west coast, small and sleepy Frederiksted is St Croix's second town. Fort Frederiksted, on the harbour, was completed in 1760, and houses a well laid-out island history museum with sections on local Crucian culture.

There are several interesting sights near by, starting with **Whim Plantation Museum**, a splendidly restored 18th-century plantation great house featuring an unusual oval-shaped interior. Its rooms have been furnished with period antiques and paintings, and they are kept refreshingly cool by 3ft-thick (1m) walls and an air moat. The plantation's old sugar mill and cane crushing gear are on view in the grounds. The **St George Village Botanical Garden** has been planted around the ruins of another former mill complex where Arawak Indians once camped. The 16-acre (6.5ha) landscaped site contains over 800 species of tropical plant, a rainforest trail and scented frangipani walk. Another very popular stop, the modern **Cruzan Rum Distillery** opens for tours, tastings and sales of its award-winning products.

St Croix Aquarium
- ✉ Caravelle Arcade
- ☎ (340) 773-8995
- 🕐 Tue–Sat 11–4
- 👆 Cheap

Buck Island
- ✉ National Park Service Dock
- ☎ (340) 773-1460
- 🕐 Daily trips at 9AM and 1PM
- 👆 Expensive

Whim Plantation Museum
- ✉ Centerline Road
- ☎ (340) 772-0598
- 🕐 Mon–Sat 10–4
- 👆 Moderate

St George Village Botanical Garden
- ✉ Centerline Road
- ☎ (340) 692-2874
- 🕐 Tue–Sat 9–4
- 👆 Moderate

Cruzan Rum Distillery
- ✉ SR64
- ☎ (340) 692-2280
- 🕐 Mon–Fri 9–11:30, 1–4:15
- 👆 Cheap

Charlotte Amalie

ℹ Tourist information
offices at Emancipation
Park in downtown
Charlotte Amalie, and
Havensight Mall

❓ Virgin Islands Carnival
(Apr)

Fort Christian

✉ Emancipation Park
☎ (340) 776-4566
⊙ Mon–Fri 8:30–4:30
👪 Cheap

Paradise Point Tramway

✉ Long Bay Road
☎ (340) 774-9809
⊙ Daily 9–5
👪 Expensive

Atlantis Submarines

✉ Havensight Mall,
Building 6
☎ (340) 776-5650
⊙ Hourly departures from
9AM
👪 Expensive

Coral World

✉ Coki Point
☎ (340) 775-1555
⊙ Daily 9–5:30
👪 Expensive

ST JOHN (▶ 25, TOP TEN)

ST THOMAS ✪✪✪

St Thomas is the administrative centre of the USVI, and one of the richest and most populous islands in the region. Some 50,000 people inhabit its hilly contours and their numbers are boosted daily by a steady flow of vacationers and cruise-ship passengers on a mission to pillage the duty-free stores of the island capital, Charlotte Amalie.

The town was declared a freeport in 1724, and its famous shopping action is concentrated between Main Street and the waterfront. On the sightseeing trail, take a look around the island history displays housed in **Fort Christian**, the harbour fortress founded in 1672. Behind the busy shopping district, a jumble of pretty houses and 19th-century public buildings climbs steeply on narrow shady streets linked by flights of steps. Heading east, there are terrific views across town from the **Paradise Point Tramway**, opposite Havensight Mall, where **Atlantis Submarines** offer popular mini-sub trips to the Buck Island Reef.

The marine park and underwater observatory at **Coral World**, near Coki Beach on the northeast coast, provides a land-based opportunity to come face to face with bizarre and brilliant marine life (▶ 109). Inland, scenic Skyline Drive follows a roller-coaster route along the central island ridge to the look-out at Drake's Seat for grand views across the neighbouring islands and a bird's-eye perspective of stunning Magens Bay, a mile-long crescent of palm-fringed sand frequently rated amongst the top ten beaches in the world. A thousand feet above the bay, the botanical gardens at the Estate St Peter Great House are another popular vantage point. The gardens can be explored on wooden boardwalk trails, and orientation boards indicate local landmarks and neighbouring islands.

The Windward Islands

The lush and lovely volcanic Windward Islands of Dominica, St Lucia, St Vincent and Grenada (► 18–19) taper south from the Leewards towards South America. Their rainforest heights and pristine dive sites are proving a major attraction for active types keen to combine the traditional sand-and-sea Caribbean holiday with a more adventurous approach.

Below: *quiet, sun-baked streets and ramshackle Creole buildings in the unassuming Dominican capital of Roseau*

DOMINICA 😊😊

Mountainous and beautiful Dominica (pronounced Domin-eeker) is known as the 'Nature Island of the Caribbean'. Its rugged topography has kept development at bay, and the island has few beaches, but it is fast gaining a reputation for activity holidays focused on its superb dive sites and challenging hikes in the highlands.

The pint-sized capital of **Roseau** lies on a small patch of flat coastal land between the Roseau River and 18th-century Fort Young (now a hotel). Set back from the waterfront, the straggling streets are lined with weather-beaten Creole buildings festooned with gingerbread decorations and flaking paint. On Old Market Place, the colonial heart of town where slave auctions were once held, the informative **Dominica Museum** traces the island's Anglo-French history, and there are sections on the few surviving Carib Indians who live on the east coast.

South of town, several hotels and dive outfits hug the shore at Castle Comfort, convenient for the nearby Scott's Head/Soufrière Bay Marine Park (► 113).

🕂 54C3
ℹ️ National Development Corporation, PO Box 293, Roseau, Commonwealth of Dominica ☎ (767) 448-2045. Also information kiosks at Canefield and Melville Hall airports
❓ Carnival (Feb, pre-Lent)

Roseau
✉️ Southwest coast
🍴 Cafés and restaurants (£–££)
ℹ️ Old Market Square

Dominica Museum
✉️ Bay Street
🕐 Mon–Fri 9–4, Sat 9–12
💷 Cheap

Morne Trois Pitons National Park
- ✉ Several trails start at Laudat
- ☎ (767) 448-2733
- 💵 Cheap for individual beauty spots within the park, and moderate daily and weekly all-area passes
- ❓ Guided hikes in the National Park and Northern Forest Reserve (► 110–11)

Cabrits National Park
- ✉ Portsmouth
- ☎ (767) 448-2401
- 🕐 Daily 8–4
- 💵 Free

A local fisherman mends his traps on the rocky shore near Scott's Head in the far south of Dominica

To the east, tucked into the rainforested recesses of the Roseau Valley, the 200ft-high (60m) Trafalgar Falls plummet down a sheer cliff face in thunderous clouds of spray to a pool where the iron-rich waters have streaked huge boulders in orange and black stripes. The falls are part of the **Morne Trois Pitons National Park**, a 17,000-acre (6,880ha) tract of Dominica's central highlands sprinkled with lakes, waterfalls, sulphur springs and, almost invariably, rain. Despite the frequent showers, this is magnificent hiking country, with a network of trails best explored with a local guide (► 110). The even larger 22,000-acre (8,900ha) Northern Forest Reserve is home to Dominica's two rare native parrot species, the Sisserou and the Jaco, which can be spotted on the jungle-cloaked slopes of Morne Diablotin (4,747ft/1,420m), the second-highest peak in the Lesser Antilles.

In the lee of Morne Diablotin, on the northwest coast, Portsmouth is Dominica's second town, but not a place to linger. However, there are a couple of low-key local diversions such as boat rides on the Indian River and the grey volcanic sand beaches of Prince Rupert Bay. Across the top of the bay, the **Cabrits National Park** occupies a narrow peninsula. The ruins of Fort Shirley, dating from 1765, are dotted around the hillside.

Overlooking the Atlantic coast between Atkinson and Castle Bruce, the Carib Territory was established in 1903. Some 3,000 descendants of the island's original Carib population live in the Territory's eight small villages, making a living from fishing, farming and traditional basket-weaving, which is sold from roadside stalls and in the craft shops of Roseau.

Southern St Lucia Drive

A day trip to Soufrière or a complete circuit of southern St Lucia, this drive combines marvellous scenery with a range of sightseeing opportunities.

From Castries, the road south scales Morne Fortune and crosses the Cul de Sac Valley. After 5 miles (8km), there is a right turn to Marigot Bay.

Marigot Bay's picture-perfect harbour inlet is a favourite movie location and yachting centre with a strip of palm-lined beach reached by a tiny ferry from the dock.

Beyond Marigot, the road snakes along above the coast, dropping down to the pretty fishing village of Anse-La-Raye and Canaries before climbing into the rainforest and emerging above Soufrière (▶ 89), with a superb vista of the Pitons.

St Lucia's most famous landmarks, Gros Piton (2,618ft/798m) and Petit Piton (2,461ft/743m) rise dramatically sheer from the shore and are thought to have been created by volcanic activity around 15,000 years ago.

From Soufrière, a steep and winding easterly route heads into the rainforest via Diamond and the 'drive-in volcano' (▶ 89). It eventually joins the more direct westerly route and continues to Vieux Fort and the Moule à Chique peninsula at the southern tip of the island. The road up the Atlantic coast to Dennery is good and comparatively fast.

Just beyond Praslin, an observation point overlooks the offshore Frigate Islands Nature Reserve. Early summer is the best time to see the magnificent frigate birds (with a wingspan of up to 8ft/2.5m) visiting their nesting grounds on the rocky outcrops.

At Dennery, the road heads inland through the banana plantions back to Castries.

Distance
65 miles (105km); 20 miles (32km) to Soufrière

Time
Allow 2 hours each way for Soufrière, or 6 hours for the circuit

Start/end point
Castries

Lunch
Hummingbird Resort (££)
✉ Soufrière
☎ (758) 459-7232

The volcanic cone of the Petit Piton towers above the village of Soufrière on St Lucia's southwest coast

GRENADA (▶ 18–19, TOP TEN)

ST LUCIA ✪✪✪

St Lucia (pronounced *Loo-sha*) is a real Caribbean beauty, from the tips of her landmark twin peaks, the Pitons, to the soft, sandy beaches fringing the northwest coast. As well as providing a visual treat, St Lucia is one of the friendliest islands around, with a famous all-comers welcome 'jump-up' street party held every Friday night in the village of Gros Islet.

The British and the French tussled over St Lucia for more than 150 years. Though Britain got the upper hand in 1814, the islanders still speak a French-based patois, and local cuisine is above average, too. Agriculture remains an important element of the island economy, with acres of banana plantations and some sugar-cane, but tourism is gradually taking over, concentrated on the Caribbean coast around Rodney Bay in the north, and the low-key southern seaside town of Soufrière.

St Lucia's rather uninspiring capital, **Castries**, was largely rebuilt after a major fire in 1948. However, the craft and produce markets near the waterfront are a good place to snap up local colour. Near by, the interior of the 1897 Cathedral of the Immaculate Conception in Derek Walcott

---

🞤 54C3

ℹ St Lucia Tourist Board, Pointe Seraphine Cruise Ship Complex (P), Box 221, Castries ☎ (758) 452-4094; web: www.st-lucia.com

❓ Carnival (pre-Lent), St Lucia International Jazz Festival (May)

Castries

🞤 West coast

🍴 Cafés (£) and several restaurants on Morne Fortune and Vigie Point (££–£££)

Above: *bunches of home-grown bananas and other fresh local produce on sale in the Castries market*

Square (named after St Lucia's Nobel Prize-winning poet) is decorated with biblical murals. Behind the town, several old Caribbean houses have been preserved on the slopes of Morne Fortune, along with the remains of 18th-century Fort Charlotte, and the Inniskilling Memorial, which commemorates the British troops who captured the hill from the French in 1796.

The popular yachting centre of Rodney Bay is St Lucia's busiest resort area. Hotels line the shore along Reduit Beach, and there are plenty of pubs and restaurants around the marina and village of Gros Islet.

Linked to the mainland by a causeway, the **Pigeon Island National Historic Park** was once a naval look-out station. British naval hero Admiral Rodney kept an eye on the French fleet from the ruins of the hilltop fort, which still affords fantastic views out to sea and down to the central highlands. An interpretation centre has been laid out in the former Officers' Mess, and there is a botanical trail around the grassy slopes.

In the shadow of the Pitons, sleepy Soufrière was St Lucia's original settlement, founded by the French in 1746. It is an excellent base for the Soufrière Marine Park (► 113), and hikes in the National Rainforest (► 111). Aside from the beach and terrific snorkelling at Anse Chastenet, the top local attraction is **La Soufrière**, the town's namesake 'drive-in volcano'. Visitors can drive to within a few hundred yards of the sinister 7-acre (3ha) crater, which bubbles with steaming sulphur hot springs. The mineral-rich brew oozes multicoloured mineral deposits and guides regale their audience with an equally colourful mixture of facts and gory stories. A rather more attractive option is the **Diamond Botanical Gardens Waterfall and Mineral Baths** set in spectacular tropical gardens. Fed by an underground spring from La Soufrière, the mineral baths were built for French troops on the orders of Louis XVI in 1785.

The eerie, steaming sulphur pits at La Soufrière

Pigeon Island National Historic Park
⊠ Pigeon Point
☎ (758) 452-5005
🕐 Daily 9–5
🍴 Café and pub (£)
👍 Cheap

La Soufrière Sulphur Springs
⊠ 3 miles (5km) east of Soufrière
🕐 Daily 9–5
👍 Free (cheap tours)

Diamond Botanical Gardens Waterfall and Mineral Baths
⊠ 2 miles (3km) east of Soufrière
🕐 Daily 10–5
👍 Cheap

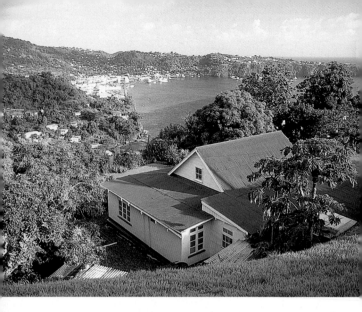

 54C2

ℹ️ St Vincent and the
Grenadines Tourist
Office, Bay Street (PO
Box 834), Kingstown
☎ (784) 457-1502; web:
www.stvincentand
grenadines.com

❓ Vincy Mas Carnival
(Jun–Jul), Nine Mornings
Festival (Dec)

Fort Charlotte
☎ (784) 456-1830
🕐 Daily dawn to dusk
🎟️ Free

Botanical Gardens
☎ (784) 457-1003
🕐 Daily dawn to dusk
🎟️ Free
❓ Cheap guided tours

*Above: a sweeping view
across Kingstown Bay
with the city occupying
centre stage sheltered by
forested hills*

ST VINCENT ⭐

Heading the 60-mile (96km) chain of the Grenadine Islands
(► 20), St Vincent is quiet, green and unassuming. Its
mountainous rainforest interior, dominated by the
grumbling Soufrière volcano (4,049ft/1,178m), once
provided sanctuary to Carib Indians and runaway slaves
whose ferocious defence of their territory kept colonists at
bay right up to the mid-18th century. Today it combines its
role as a staging post for sailing holidays and diving excursions (► 113) in the Grenadines with a low-key
eco-tourism programme, attracting hikers and bird-
watchers (► 110–11).

Sandwiched between the mountains and the sea,
Kingstown is the capital of St Vincent and the Grenadines.
The town centre has retained its old arcaded sidewalks,
the parliament building and several imposing churches
dating from colonial days. Down-island ferries depart from
the busy waterfront, and there are splendid views across
to the Grenadines chain from the battlements of **Fort
Charlotte**, perched on the western rim of the bay.
Kingstown's **Botanical Gardens** are the oldest of their
kind in the western hemisphere, founded in 1765. Guides
will point out some of the more bizarre and interesting
specimens, and particular pride is taken in the breadfruit
trees, descended from original specimens introduced to
the Caribbean by Captain Bligh in 1793.

Most visitors stay in the vicinity of Villa, a 20-minute
drive east of the capital. Popular excursions include the
beautiful, emerald green hills of the Mesopotamia Valley,
St Vincent's agricultural heartland, and day sails to the Falls
of Baleine, which tumble down the slopes of La Soufrière
on the north coast.

Where To...

Above: *cruise ships at Heritage Quay, Antigua*
Right: *a doll in traditional Creole dress*

Western Caribbean

Prices

Prices are approximate, based on a three-course meal for one without drinks and service:

£ = under US$20
££ = US$20–40
£££ = over US$40

Bahamas

Fatman's Nephew (£)

Outdoor terrace overlooking the marina, with relaxed atmosphere and generous platters of Bahamanian favourites such as cracked conch, burgers and curries.

✉ **Port Lucaya Marketplace, Grand Bahama** ☎ (242) 373-8520 🕐 **Lunch, dinner**

Graycliff (£££)

Arguably the best dining-room on the island, set in a gracious 250-year-old mansion. Continental and Bahamian cuisine, magnificent wine cellar and polished formal service. Reservations.

✉ **West Hill Street, Nassau, New Providence** ☎ (242) 322-2796 🕐 **Lunch, dinner**

Green Shutters (££)

Cosily panelled pub-restaurant serving very British pies, bangers and mash, and Bahamanian seafood dishes.

✉ **48 Parliament Street, Nassau, New Providence** ☎ (242) 325-5702 🕐 **Lunch, dinner**

Kaptain Kenny's (£)

Good base for a day on the beach, with a range of watersports served up alongside local seafood dishes, salads and grills.

✉ **Taino Beach, Grand Bahama** ☎ (242) 373-8689 🕐 **Lunch, dinner**

Cayman Islands

Cracked Conch (££)

An island institution where conch is king (chowders, fritters and more), but pastas and grills get a look in. Very popular Caribbean Sunday brunch.

✉ **West Bay, Grand Cayman** ☎ (345) 945-5217 🕐 **Lunch, dinner**

Lantanas (£££)

Imaginative Caribbean cuisine with a nod to the American southwest. Jerk pork with black beans, lobster quesadillas, apple pie and ice-cream.

✉ **Caribbean Club, West Bay Road, Seven Mile Beach, Grand Cayman** ☎ (345) 945-5595 🕐 **Lunch (weekdays only), dinner**

Dominican Republic

Casa del Río (££)

Atmospheric Old World-style setting with vertiginous views over the Chavón Valley and an elegantly presented French-Continental menu.

✉ **Altos de Chavón** ☎ (809) 523-3333 🕐 **Lunch, dinner**

El Conuco (£)

Entertaining local restaurant with a rustic theme, thatched roof and assortment of tools and utensils tacked to the walls. Good food; singing-dancing staff.

✉ **Calle Casimiro de Moya 152, Santo Domingo** ☎ (809) 686-0129 🕐 **Lunch, dinner**

Puntilla de Pierforgio (££)

Italian restaurant renowned for its classic pasta and seafood dishes. Alfresco dining on a series of clifftop terraces overlooking the ocean.

✉ **Calle La Puntilla, Sosúa** ☎ (809) 571-2215 🕐 **Lunch, dinner**

Vesuvio I (£££)

A long-established family-run Italian restaurant on the

Malecón with a jolly atmosphere and plenty of Caribbean seafood specials mixed in among the classic veal and pasta dishes.

✉ **Avenida George Washington 1521, Santo Domingo**
☎ **(809) 221-3333** 🕐 **Lunch, dinner**

Jamaica
Blue Lagoon (£)
Famous waterfront bar set right on the Blue Lagoon. Drink in the view and dine on spicy jerk dishes, seafood and pizzas. Live music at weekends.

✉ **Fairy Hill, Port Antonio**
☎ **(876) 993-8491** 🕐 **Lunch, dinner**

Evita's (££)
Cheery Italian restaurant in an old gingerbread house, with outdoor seating and views. House specialities include home-made pastas and an enormous choice of desserts.

✉ **Eden Bower Road, Ocho Rios** ☎ **(876) 974-2333**
🕐 **Lunch, dinner**

Hungry Lion (££)
A tiny oasis of hippy-dom and abundant tropical flora. Terrific vegetarian/vegan and seafood menu at night; snacks and exotic fruit juices during the day.

✉ **West End Road, Negril**
☎ **(876) 957-4330**
🕐 **Dinner**

Pork Pit (£)
Hot, hot, hot jerk pork, chicken and ribs (Jamaica's national dish, ➤ 94 panel) served with rice 'n' peas, cornbread, cold beers and other local staples. Picnic benches catch the breeze off Walter Fletcher Beach.

✉ **Gloucester Avenue, Montego Bay** ☎ **(876) 952-1046**
🕐 **Lunch, dinner**

Rick's Café (££)
The sunset party spot in Negril, Rick's also has a popular terrace restaurant offering all the usual suspects from broiled Caribbean lobster to fresh fruit daiquiris.

✉ **West End Road, Negril**
☎ **(876) 957-4200** 🕐 **Lunch, dinner**

Round Hill Hotel (£££)
Elegant Georgian-style dining pavilion overlooking the sea in Jamaica's top hotel. The finest local ingredients and recipes combined with continental flair; historic Jamaican buffets (Mon and Fri, ££).

✉ **8 miles (13km) west of Montego Bay** ☎ **(876) 952-5150**
🕐 **Breakfast, lunch, dinner**

Puerto Rico
Ajili Mojili (££)
Bustling and popular dining-room specialising in hearty Puerto Rican cooking. Scrumptious assorted fritters (corn, pumpkin, cheese) followed by swordfish, beef or skewered pork.

✉ **1052 Ashford Avenue, Condado, San Juan**
☎ **(787) 725-9195** 🕐 **Lunch Mon–Fri, dinner**

Amadeus (££)
Relaxed yet chic spot with a wide-ranging Nouvelle Caribbean menu. Plantain mousse with shrimp, chicken breast stuffed with snails and mushrooms.

✉ **Calle San Sebastián 106, Old San Juan** ☎ **(787) 722-8635** 🕐 **Lunch, dinner. Closed Mon**

Yucca and Yams
Spanish settlers in the West Caribbean picked up several gastronomic ingredients from the native Taino Indians including yuccas, yams and cassava flour. In the Dominican Republic and Puerto Rico, these starchy staples can be found in many hearty local dishes. Fresh seafood and Spanish-influenced chicken and rice dishes are popular, and there is plenty of pork, from *chicharrón* (similar to pork scratchings) and *tortilla de jamon* (ham omelette) to *lechón asao* (suckling pig). Somewhat less appealing, *mondongo* (tripe stew) is a popular hangover cure in the Dominican Republic.

Western & Eastern Caribbean

Jerk

Synonymous with Jamaica, jerked meats and fish cooked in a barbecue pit are now popular throughout the Caribbean. Arawak Indians gave the word 'barbecue' to the world, and the original recipe for jerk was supposedly concocted by Jamaican Maroons, runaway slaves who took to the hills and cooked over earth pits covered with branches from pepper and allspice trees. Herbs such as nutmeg and wild thyme have since been added to the spicy seasoning and jerk has become a Caribbean culinary classic.

La Bombonera (£)

An old-fashioned local restaurant and snack stop offering hearty, no-frills Puerto Rican food such as soups, omelettes, seafood and rice dishes.

✉ Calle San Francisco 259, Old San Juan ☎ (787) 772-0658 🕐 Breakfast, lunch, dinner

Chef Marisoll (£££)

Marisoll Hernandez's imaginative contemporary cuisine has earned considerable acclaim. Sample tuna steak with honey-soy sauce or grouper Creole. Reservations.

✉ Calle Del Cristo 202, Old San Juan ☎ (787) 725-7454 🕐 Lunch Tue–Sat, dinner Tue–Sun

Horned Dorset Primavera (£££)

Beachfront location and sophisticated continental cuisine with Caribbean accents such as shrimp and fennel bisque, and grilled marlin with fresh herbs. Reservations essential.

✉ Apartado 1132, 6 miles (10km) northwest of Mayaguez ☎ (787) 823-4030 🕐 Lunch, dinner

Pito's Seafood (££)

A breezy seafront terrace just outside town and the freshest local seafood make for a great lunch stop. Stuffed clams, grilled mahi-mahi, lobster and snapper.

✉ Route 2, Las Cucharas, Ponce ☎ (787) 841-4977 🕐 Lunch, dinner

Eastern Caribbean

Barbados
Atlantis Hotel (£)

The set-price lunch at the Atlantis's clifftop restaurant makes a great stop on a round-island tour. Sunday's West Indian buffet is a local legend; reservations essential.

✉ Bathsheba ☎ (246) 433-9445 🕐 Lunch, dinner. Closed Sun dinner

The Cliff (£££)

Stunning alfresco dining on terraces cut into the cliffs. Light, sophisticated cuisine, excellent wine list and a suitably fashionable clientele.

✉ Derricks ☎ (246) 432-1922 🕐 Dinner

Pisces (££)

Popular and pretty multi-level dining-room on the water's edge. Tasty seafood dishes include shrimp and tomato stuffed snapper, or there are chicken and pasta options.

✉ St Lawrence Gap ☎ (246) 435-6564 🕐 Dinner

French Antilles
Fishpot (£££)

A formal candle-lit bastion of gourmet excellence. Terrace dining overlooking the beach, classic French-Caribbean cuisine such as duck breast cooked in mature rum; elegant vegetarian options.

✉ 82 boulevard de Grand Case, Grand Case, St-Martin ☎ (590) 87-50-88 🕐 Dinner

La Fontane (£££)

Gourmet French-Creole dining-room in a lovely old hillside home above Fort-de-France. Try the lobster ragoût with basil, or noisettes of lamb with mango sauce.

✉ Rue de Balata, La Fontane, Martinique ☎ (596) 64-28-70 🕐 Lunch, dinner. Closed Sun–Mon

Le Karacoli (£–££)
Popular lunch stop on a round-island tour. Beachfront position and good-value set-price menus with pricier à la carte suggestions. Creole specialities and seafood.

✉ Grande Anse, Basse-Terre, Guadeloupe ☎ (590) 28-41-17 🕐 Lunch

Au Poisson d'Or (££)
Lively Creole restaurant with waitresses in traditional costume. Local delicacies include conch marinated in lime juice, grilled lobster Creole and spicy shark.

✉ Anse Mitan, Trois Ilets, Martinique ☎ (596) 66-01-80 🕐 Lunch (high season only), dinner. Closed Mon, Jul

Le Vieux Port (££)
Cosy wooden shack facing the seafront with a mouth-watering menu of fish soups and stews, crayfish with ginger and coconut, and local lobster.

✉ St François, Grande-Terre, Guadeloupe ☎ (590) 88-46-60 🕐 Lunch, dinner

Leeward Islands
Admiral's Inn (££)
Welcoming historic inn with a shady terrace overlooking the harbour. Good choice of salads, grilled fish and omelettes at lunch; more substantial evening meals.

✉ Nelson's Dockyard, English Harbour, Antigua ☎ (268) 460-1027 🕐 Lunch, dinner

Ballahoo (££)
Handy central meeting place in the upper storey of an old town house. Sandwiches, burgers and salads for lunch; chilli shrimp, fish steaks and pasta in the evening. Vegetarian choices.

✉ The Circus, Basseterre, St Kitts ☎ (869) 465-9927 🕐 Breakfast, lunch, dinner. Closed Sun

Blanchard's (£££)
Beachfront tropical elegance and sophisticated New American-Asian cuisine delivering delicacies such as lemon-glazed lobster dumplings. Award-winning wine list.

✉ Mead's Bay, Anguilla ☎ (264) 497-6100 🕐 Dinner. Closed Sun

Golden Lemon (££)
Delightful historic inn with good food – omelettes, salads and fresh fish for lunch; tasty warm fish salad and grilled lamb with garlic, lemon and coriander for dinner.

✉ Dieppe Bay, St Kitts ☎ (869) 465-7260 🕐 Lunch, dinner

Hermitage Inn (£–££)
Relaxed and welcoming plantation house hotel serving lunch on the terrace. Generous lobster salad platter, rotis, home-baked bread. There is also a very good set-price dinner menu (££).

✉ Gingerland, Nevis ☎ (869) 469-3477 🕐 Breakfast, lunch, dinner

Julian's (£££)
Cosy dining-room in an old colonial home. Delicious classical-modern cooking with local touches. Butternut soup, roulade of pork and roasted plantain; snapper ceviche; long wine list.

✉ Church Street at Corn Alley, St John's, Antigua ☎ (268) 462-4766 🕐 Dinner. Closed Mon

Vegetarians
The idea of being rich enough to eat meat but electing not to is a bizarre one for many Caribbean islanders. It is relatively easy to avoid red meat in favour of fish and seafood, but unadulterated vegetable dishes (with the exception of uninspiring mixed salads) are harder to find. Rastafarian cooking offers the best option if you can find it. I-Tal, as it is called, uses only natural ingredients, no meat, salt or alcohol, and in many cases no dairy products.

Going Dutch

Dining out in the Dutch ABCs there are several culinary surprises in store. Traditional Dutch cheeses such as Edam and Gouda pop up in *pastechi* (turnovers) and other savoury dishes. Authentic local dishes include *stoba di yuana* (iguana stew), or *storba di cani* (meat, often goat, stew) accompanied by a slab of *funchi* (boiled maize, rather like polenta). The former Dutch colony of Indonesia has added *rijstaffel* to the local lexicon. These multi-course Asian feasts make a fun night out.

Mango's (££)

Pretty courtyard shaded by a giant mango tree. Broad menu including goat's cheese salads, Thai shrimp curry and exotic fruit ice-creams. Live music and busy bar Fri nights.

✉ **Independence Square, Basseterre, St Kitts** ☎ **(869) 465-4049** ⏰ **Lunch, dinner. Closed Sun**

Pizzas in Paradise (££)

Pizzas, sandwiches, salads, cold drinks and cappuccinos in an old brick warehouse at the heart of the downtown shopping district.

✉ **Redcliffe Quay, St John's, Antigua** ☎ **(268) 462-2621** ⏰ **Lunch, dinner. Closed Sun**

Netherlands Antilles

Bistro Le Clochard (£££)

A former fortress gaol transformed into a cosy dining-room. Swiss fondues are a house speciality, along with sizzling beef cooked on a stone slab. Rich desserts and fine wines.

✉ **Riffort, Otrobanda, Willenstad, Curaçao** ☎ **(5999) 462-5666** ⏰ **Lunch (except Sat), dinner**

Boonoonoonoos (££)

The name means 'extraordinary' in Jamaican *patois* and the food is stylish Caribbean, from the jerk ribs to the Carib Combo taster platter showcasing regional specialities.

✉ **Wilhelminastraat 18A, Oranjestad, Aruba** ☎ **(297) 831888** ⏰ **Lunch (except Sun), dinner**

Jaanchie's (£)

Casual local restaurant with a shady terrace ideal for a lunch break on an island tour. Salads and seafood as well as traditional goat or iguana *stobas* (stews).

✉ **Westpunt, Curaçao** ☎ **(5999) 864-0126** ⏰ **Lunch**

Kangaroo Court Caffe (£)

Handy town-centre pit-stop with a leafy courtyard for generous breakfasts, coffee and pastries, deli sandwiches, ice-creams and frozen yogurts.

✉ **Hendrik Gevangenistreeg, Philipsburg, Sint Maarten** ⏰ **Breakfast, lunch. Closed Sun**

Papiamento (£££)

Intimate family-run restaurant in the gardens of a 150-year-old manor house. Award-winning seafood, steaks and admirably tempting healthy and vegetarian dishes.

✉ **Washington 61, Oranjestad, Aruba** ☎ **(297) 864544** ⏰ **Dinner. Closed Sun**

Richard's Waterfront (££)

Settle down with a sunset cocktail and peruse the blackboard menu for fresh local seafood or the chef's signature chicken Benito with spinach and Dutch cheese.

✉ **J A Abraham Boulevard, Playa Pariba, Bonaire** ☎ **(5997) 5263** ⏰ **Dinner. Closed Mon**

Seafood Gallery (££)

Nautical New England-style establishment on the water boasting a raw bar and an enormous selection of baked, grilled, stewed and sauced fresh fish and seafood.

✉ **Bobby's Marina, Philipsburg, Sint Maarten**

☎ (5995) 23253 ⏱ **Lunch, dinner. Closed Sun**

Zeezicht Bonaire (£–££)
Large American breakfasts, grilled fish sandwiches and burgers, plus a more adventurous dinner menu with several Indonesian specialities.
✉ **Kaya J N E Craane 12, Kralendijk, Bonaire** ☎ **(5997) 8438** ⏱ **Breakfast, lunch, dinner**

Trinidad & Tobago
Jemma's Sea View Kitchen (£)
A handful of tables on decks balanced above the shore and Jemma's simple but hearty fish and chicken dishes make this a popular stop on island tours. Soft drinks only.
✉ **Windward Road, Speyside, Tobago** ☎ **(868) 660-4066** ⏱ **Lunch, dinner. Closed Fri dinner–Sat**

Shirvan Watermill (££)
Romantic, cleverly lit garden pavilion situated by an old mill. Try the elegantly presented mushrooms stuffed with crabmeat, honey duck and grilled freshwater crayfish.
✉ **Leeward Road, Mount Pleasant, Tobago** ☎ **(868) 639-0000** ⏱ **Dinner**

Solimar (££)
Pretty veranda dining area with a broad range of international flavours from swordfish gravlax with saffron-Dijon mustard dressing to Indonesian spicy beef.
✉ **6 Nook Avenue, St Ann's, Port of Spain, Trinidad** ☎ **(868) 624-6267** ⏱ **Dinner. Closed Sun, and Mon Mar–Nov**

Veni Mangé (£)
There is a big local following for this fun restaurant run by a local chat show hostess and her sister. Creative Nouvelle Caribbean cooking and vegetarian dishes feature here.
✉ **67A Ariapata Avenue, Woodbrook, Port of Spain, Trinidad** ☎ **(868) 624-4597** ⏱ **Lunch, dinner (Wed only). Closed Sat and Sun**

British Virgin Islands
Olde Yard Inn (£–££)
Charming small inn serving a selection of light lunches at the poolside Sip & Dip Grill. A more substantial evening menu offers local and international dishes from garlicky snails to Caribbean lobster.
✉ **The Valley, Virgin Gorda** ☎ **(284) 495-5544** ⏱ **Breakfast, lunch, dinner**

Quito's Gazebo (£–££)
Quito's is a casual and friendly beach bar-restaurant with live music on weekends and occasional impromptu week nights. Burgers and sandwiches, grilled fish, pasta and pecan pie are some of the options.
✉ **Cane Garden Bay, Tortola** ☎ **(284) 495-4837** ⏱ **Lunch, dinner**

Sugar Mill (££)
The Sugar Mill has atmospheric old stone walls decorated with Haitian art, and a small but delicately balanced daily menu including the likes of sweet potato soup with gingered shrimp and tropical game hen.
✉ **Apple Bay, Tortola** ☎ **(284) 495-4355** ⏱ **Lunch, dinner**

Captain Bligh and the Breadfruit
Better known for surviving mutiny on the high seas, Captain Bligh played an important role in Caribbean culinary history. In 1793 he imported breadfruit from the South Pacific as a cheap and nutritious foodstuff for slaves on the sugar plantations. At first the slaves refused to eat the strange vegetable, but soon it became a dietary staple and towering, glossy-leafed breadfruit trees now flourish throughout the region.

Breakfast at Dowies

Sisters Anna Doward and Daphne Davis cook up a storm in their tiny kitchen on St Croix, and Friday's traditional Crucian breakfast is set to become an island institution. Saltfish prepared with onions and peppers is the order of the day, accompanied by thick wedges of fried johnnycake (bread). Lunchtime specials might include conch in butter sauce, *souse* (pork stew with lime), or their award-winning fish pudding washed down with a glass of *maubi* made from tree bark and herbs (and something of an acquired taste).

US Virgin Islands

Asolare (£££)

One of St John's top dining experiences, plus superb views over Cruz Bay. Asian-Pacific Rim cuisine laced with a few more classical continental dishes and seafood specialities.

✉ **North Shore Road, St John** ☎ **(340) 779-4747** ⓘ **Dinner**

Blue Moon (££)

Casual bistro with indoor and outdoor seating and an eclectic menu featuring dishes such as Cajun shrimp and spicy Creole chicken. Live jazz Fri night and Sun brunch.

✉ **17 Strand Street, Frederiksted, St Croix** ☎ **(340) 772-2222** ⓘ **Lunch, dinner. Closed Mon and Sat lunch, Sun–Mon dinner**

Cuzzins' Caribbean Restaurant (£)

Terrific local menu of soups, stews and curries with plenty of tasty side dishes. Delicious fresh juices; charming service.

✉ **7 Back Street, Charlotte Amalie, St Thomas** ☎ **(340) 777-4711** ⓘ **Lunch, dinner. Closed Tue dinner, Sun**

Dowies (£)

Tiny outdoor café, great for sampling traditional Crucian cooking (► panel).

✉ **111 Market Street, Frederiksted, St Croix** ☎ **(340) 772-0845** ⓘ **Breakfast, lunch. Closed Mon**

Fish Trap (££)

Informal alfresco restaurant with a big local following. Daily fresh fish specials, grilled steaks, pastas and wicked home-made desserts.

✉ **Raintree Inn, Cruz Bay, St John** ☎ **(340) 693-9994** ⓘ **Lunch, dinner. Closed Mon**

Hervé (£££)

Sweeping harbour views compliment a chic French-American menu. Salade Niçoise and other lighter lunch options; steaks and seafood predominate at night. Reservations.

✉ **Government Hill, Charlotte Amalie, St Thomas** ☎ **(340) 777-9703** ⓘ **Lunch, dinner**

Indies (££)

Attractive courtyard setting for stylish California-Caribbean cooking which includes grilled vegetable antipasto, blackened fish and spice-rubbed duck with pineapple chutney.

✉ **55–6 Company Street, Christiansted, St Croix** ☎ **(340) 692-9440** ⓘ **Lunch Mon–Fri, dinner**

Sprat Hall Beach Restaurant (££)

Informal lunch stop right on the sand, ideal for a break and a swim. Try the pumpkin fritters, fresh fish, salads or burgers. Beach loungers and changing facilities available.

✉ **Route 63, 1 mile (1.5km) north of Frederiksted, St Croix** ☎ **(340) 772-5855** ⓘ **Lunch**

Wahoo Willy's (££)

Waterfront location with a long menu of burgers, pizzas and salads for lunch and more substantial seafood and steak dishes in the evening.

✉ **Hotel Caravelle, 44A Queen Cross Street, Christiansted, St Croix** ☎ **(340) 773-6585** ⓘ **Lunch, dinner**

WHERE TO EAT & DRINK

Zorba's (££)

Popular and fun Greek restaurant dishing up all the old favourites from houmous and taramasalata dips to vine-wrapped *dolmas* and lamb. Also a selection of vegetarian options.

✉ Government Hill, Charlotte Amalie, St Thomas ☎ (340) 776-0444 🕐 Lunch, dinner. Closed Sun lunch

Windward Islands

Coconuts' Beach Restaurant (££)

This quaint wooden cottage, right on the beach, combined with assured French–Creole cooking, is a winning combination. Crêpes, curries and the catch of the day.

✉ Grand Anse Beach, Grenada ☎ (473) 444-4644 🕐 Lunch, dinner (except Tue)

Dasheen (££–£££)

Magnificent clifftop position with views of the Pitons and imaginative Creole-international cuisine. Chilled seafood in gazpacho, scallops braised in coconut milk and ginger.

✉ Ladera Resort (south of Soufrière), St Lucia ☎ (758) 459-7323 🕐 Breakfast, lunch, dinner

Morne Fendue (£)

An island institution renowned for its pepperpot (▶ panel) and West Indian lunch buffet.

✉ Southeast of Sauteurs, Grenada ☎ (473) 442-9330 🕐 Lunch. Closed Sun

Papillote Wilderness Retreat (£–££)

Only the freshest local ingredients are used to create the simple but tasty dishes served in this rain-forest inn close to the Trafalgar Falls.

✉ Trafalgar Valley, Dominica ☎ (767) 448-2287 🕐 Lunch, dinner (reservations)

La Robe Creole (££)

Charming Creole restaurant in an historic town house. The seasonal selection of local dishes might include spicy stuffed land crabs and 'mountain chicken' (frogs' legs).

✉ 3 Victoria Street, Roseau, Dominica ☎ (767) 448-2896 🕐 Lunch, dinner. Closed Sun

Snooty Agouti (££)

Cheerful attic dining-room decorated with hanging plants, brightly checked table cloths and local art. The eclectic menu covers all the bases from moussaka to crab cakes.

✉ Gros Islet, St Lucia ☎ (758) 452-0321 🕐 Breakfast, lunch, dinner

St Vincent & the Grenadines

French Restaurant (££)

Authentic French owners and an impressive seafood menu (big on lobster). Steaks and beef fillet with wonderful sauces, Burgundian snails, alcoholic coffees.

✉ Villa, St Vincent ☎ (784) 458-4972 🕐 Lunch, dinner. Closed Sun

Gingerbread (£–££)

A café for coffees, juices and home-baked cakes; a lunchtime barbecue; and a pretty restaurant with harbour views serving soups, salads, pasta and excellent curries.

✉ Port Elizabeth, Bequia ☎ (784) 458-3800 🕐 Lunch, dinner

Pepperpot

A good pepperpot, a savoury meat and vegetable stew constantly replenished with fresh ingredients, never runs out. The pepperpot at Morne Fendue in Grenada has achieved legendary status, though the present incarnation only dates back to 1984 after its even older predecessor was killed off during political upheavals. Pepperpot forms the centrepiece of Morne Fendue's lunchtime buffet, alongside callaloo soup, baked chicken, fish, roasted breadfruit and plantain, christophene gratin and other Windward Island favourites.

Western Caribbean

Prices
Prices are based on a standard double room during the high season (► panel opposite), excluding breakfast and taxes:

£ = under US$150
££ = US$150–$250
£££ = over US$250

The Bahamas
Bahamas Princess Resort & Casino (££)
A huge low-rise resort with excellent sports facilities, children's programmes and Las Vegas-style shows in the casino.

✉ Freeport, Grand Bahama ☎ (242) 352-6721; fax (242) 352-6842

Compass Point Beach Club (££)
Eighteen cute clapboard beach cottages, hip clientele, on-site dive shop and watersports. Good bar and restaurant.

✉ Love Beach, New Providence ☎ (242) 327-4500; fax (242) 327-3299

Cayman Islands
Sunset House (££)
Notable small and friendly dive hotel with good shore diving, scuba and underwater photography tuition. Lively bar for sunset cocktails.

✉ George Town, Grand Cayman ☎ (345) 949-7111; fax (345) 949-7101

Dominican Republic
Casa Bonita (£)
Charming country-style inn set in the hills above a stretch of unspoilt coastline. Spotless and comfortable; restaurant and bar.

✉ Bahoruca, Barahona ☎ (809) 696-0215; fax (809) 223-0548

Rancho Baiguate (£)
Adventure sports centre in the central highlands with simple accommodation and a host of activities including hiking, canyoning, rafting and mountain- and quad-biking.

✉ Jarabacoa ☎ (809) 574-6890; fax (809) 574-4940

Jamaica
Hibiscus Lodge Hotel (££)
Intimate and charming inn set in pretty gardens, with some rooms on cliffside terraces. Pool, tennis and the renowned Almond Tree restaurant.

✉ 83 Main Street, Ocho Rios ☎ (876) 974-2676; fax (876) 974-1874

Jake's (£)
Funky beach cottages in an eclectic mix of Jamaican, Mexican and Catalan styles with ceiling fans and outdoor showers. Good local food.

✉ Treasure Beach ☎ /fax (876) 965-0552

Strawberry Hill (£££)
Quiet and stylish mountain retreat. All 12 garden villas have vast four-poster beds, plantation-style furnishings, kitchens and private verandas. Fine dining; spa.

✉ Irish Town ☎ (876) 993-8491; fax (876) 993-8492

Puerto Rico
Casa Grande (£)
Peaceful small hotel in a stunning mountain setting. Twenty simple rooms with private balcony and hammock. Restaurant; hiking trails.

✉ Route 612 (KM0.3), Utuado ☎ (787) 894-3939; fax (787) 894-3900

El Convento (££–£££)
Characterful lodgings in upper storeys of a 17th-century convent, with antique Spanish décor, plunge pool with harbour views, and shops and restaurants below.

✉ Calle Cristo 100, Old San Juan ☎ (787) 723-9020; fax (787) 721-2877

Eastern Caribbean

Barbados

Sandy Lane (£££)
Arguably the most famous and glamorous hotel in the Caribbean, the Sandy Lane is undergoing a major face-lift and aims to reopen sometime in the year 2000.
✉ **Payne's Bay, St James Parish** ☎ **(246) 432-1311; fax (246) 432-2954**

Woodville Beach (£)
Friendly, family-run business with large, good-value studios and one- to two-bedroom self-catering apartments close to the beach.
✉ **Hastings, Christ Church Parish** ☎ **(246) 435-6694; fax (246) 435-9211**

French Antilles

Diamant Les Bain (£)
Relaxed and welcoming family-run concern right on the beach. Bright, simple rooms and garden cottages. Watersports, diving, tennis and horse-riding near by.
✉ **Bourg du Diamant, Martinique** ☎ **(596) 76-40-14; fax (596) 76-27-00**

Habitation Lagrange (£££)
Peaceful and romantic hideaway in the forest. Antique-filled rooms in the lovely 1850s estate house with gardens, 30 minutes from beach. Tennis, pool.
✉ **Le Marigot, Martinique** ☎ **(596) 53-60-60; fax (596) 53-50-58**

Le Hamak (£££)
Guadeloupe's most exclusive and luxurious hotel. Stylish garden cottages with private patios and namesake hammocks. Gourmet dining and attentive service.
✉ **St François, Grande-Terre, Guadeloupe** ☎ **(590) 88-59-99; fax (590) 88-41-92**

Hévéa (£)
Delightful Creole inn across from the beach. Choice of attractive rooms, studios and apartments, some with four-posters.
✉ **163 boulevard de Grand Case, Grand Case, St-Martin** ☎ **(590) 878-56-85; fax (590) 87-83-88**

Relais de Moulin (£)
Small, family-friendly resort with self-catering bungalows in gardens around an old windmill east of Ste Anne. Ten minutes' walk from the beach; bicycles, tennis and riding.
✉ **Châteaubrun, Grande-Terre, Guadeloupe** ☎ **(590) 88-23-96; fax (590) 88-03-93**

Le Toiny (£££)
Fabulous Relais et Châteaux property offering a dozen luxury cottages with private pools. Gourmet dining.
✉ **Anse de Toiny, St-Barthélemy** ☎ **(590) 27-88-88; fax (590) 27-89-30**

Leeward Islands

Anguilla Great House (££)
Unpretentious spot with 27 simple, spacious gingerbread cottages and a bar-restaurant on a fabulous beach.
✉ **Rendezvous Bay, Anguilla** ☎ **(264) 497-6061; fax (264) 497-6019**

Curtain Bluff (£££)
Antigua's most famous and elegant hotel with the best rooms/apartments perched on a bluff above the ocean. Top-notch sports facilities and gourmet dining.
✉ **Morris Bay, Antigua** ☎ **(268) 462-8400; fax (268) 462-8409**

Seasonal Variations
Room prices fall dramatically outside the main winter season in the Caribbean. Hotels command top rates from mid-December until April. There is a slight drop in prices during May and the November to mid-December seasons, while summer rates can plummet by as much as 50 per cent. It is well worth bargaining if you have not paid for accommodation in the off-season, though prices will go up temporarily at Carnival and festival times.

Hidden Extras

The rates used as the basis for the price ratings in this guide do not include assorted surcharges which may appear on the final bill. Additional government taxes can add anything between 5 and 15 per cent to the room rate, and some hotels also add an overall service charge as well as automatic 'gratuities' for drinks at the bar, restaurant meals and room service charged to the room account. Always check hotel policy in advance to avoid nasty surprises.

Montpelier Plantation Inn (£££)

Gracious hideaway with comfortable, airy garden cottages. Drinks and meals are served English country house-style in the old estate house. Tennis, pool, beach shuttle.

✉ Fig Tree, Nevis ☎ (869) 469-3462; fax (869) 469-2932

Ottley's Plantation Inn (£££)

Lovely plantation inn with beautifully furnished rooms in the 18th-century main house, and cottages in the grounds. Shuttle to the beach; good food.

✉ Ottley's, St Kitts ☎ (869) 465-7234; fax (869) 465-4760

Netherlands Antilles
All West Apartments & Diving (£)

Bright and basic studios and self-catering apartments with sea views on the quiet north coast. The friendly young owners offer dive packages.

✉ Banda Abao, Westpunt, Curaçao ☎ (5999) 864-0102; fax (5999) 461-2315

Avila Beach (££)

Charming historic hotel in a former governor's residence set in waterfront gardens. Newer rooms are particularly attractive. Tennis; fine dining.

✉ Penstraat 130, Willemstad, Curaçao ☎ (5999) 461-4377; fax (5999) 461-1493

Captain's Quarters (£)

Pleasant old inn; most rooms (with views and four-posters) in newer blocks. Gardens, good food and friendly atmosphere.

✉ Windwardside, Saba ☎ (5994) 62201; fax (5994) 62377

Capt Don's Habitat (££)

Casual and fun dive hotel with comfy rooms and cottages, excellent scuba facilities, and weekly chats from Captain Don, Bonaire's diving pioneer.

✉ Kaya Gobernador N. Debrot 85, Playa Pabao, Bonaire ☎ (5997) 8290; fax (5997) 8240

Pasanggrahan Royal Inn (£)

Historic inn in the town centre. Quiet, stylishly refurbished rooms with four-posters, and bay views from the balcony. Garden restaurant.

✉ Front Street, Philipsburg, Sint Maarten ☎ (5995) 23588; fax (5995) 22885

Trinidad & Tobago
Asa Wright Nature Centre (££)

No-frills accommodation high in the famous rainforest nature reserve. All meals included; guided field trips extra.

✉ Arima, Trinidad ☎ (868) 667-4655; fax (868) 667-4540

Footprints Eco Resort (£)

Terrific Robinson Crusoe-style thatched tree-houses with 20th-century comforts, including some solar-heated jacuzzis. Hiking and snorkelling; restaurant.

✉ Culloden Bay, Tobago ☎ (868) 660-0118; fax (868) 660-0027

British Virgin Islands
Bitter End Yacht Club (£££)

Friendly ambience, excellent yachting facilities and sailing school. Villas and romantic thatched huts on stilts, open to the breeze.

✉ North Sound, Virgin Gorda ☎ (284) 494-2746; fax (284) 494-4756

Lighthouse Villas (££)
Spacious and bright self-catering accommodation with balconies overlooking the bay. Close to beach, restaurants and bars.
✉ **Cane Garden Bay, Tortola** ☎ **(284) 494-5482; fax (284) 495-9101**

US Virgin Islands
Caneel Bay Resort (£££)
Glorious low-key Rockefeller-designed resort on seven secluded beaches. Rooms and rustic-chic cottages.
✉ **Caneel Bay, St John** ☎ **(340) 776-6111; fax (340) 693-8280**

Hilty House Inn (£)
Charming hilltop B&B set in tropical gardens with a relaxed Mediterranean feel. Four rooms and two self-catering cottages, pool deck.
✉ **Gallows Bay, St Croix** ☎ **/fax (340) 773-2594**

Hotel 1829 (££)
Historic town-centre inn. Lots of character; tiny courtyard pool and restaurant.
✉ **Government Hill, Charlotte Amalie, St Thomas** ☎ **(340) 776-1829; fax (340) 776-4313**

Windward Islands
Anchorage Hotel & Dive Centre (£)
Comfy modern units with balconies on the waterfront. PADI dive facilities and hiking trips.
✉ **Castle Comfort, Dominica** ☎ **(767) 448-2638; fax (767) 448-5680**

Anse Chastanet Beach Hotel (£££)
Great setting on a steep-sided beach cove, with excellent diving in the bay. Quaint rooms in octagonal gazebos or beachfront

suites. Very relaxing.
✉ **Soufrière, St Lucia** ☎ **(758) 459-7232; fax (758) 459-7033**

Calabash (£££)
Attractive beachfront property with wonderful service and good food. Very comfortable suites, some with private plunge pools.
✉ **L'Anse aux Epines, Grenada** ☎ **(473) 444-4334; fax (473) 444-5050**

Harmony Marina Suites (£)
Small, well-priced family-run complex minutes from Reduit Beach. Standard and deluxe units; some with four-posters, some with kitchenettes.
✉ **Rodney Bay, St Lucia** ☎ **(758) 452-8756; fax (758) 452-8677**

La Sagesse Nature Centre (£)
Appealing beach retreat with airy modern rooms in a 1920s estate house and wooden cottages on the sand. Restaurant.
✉ **La Sagesse, Grenada** ☎ **/fax (473) 444-6458**

St Vincent and the Grenadines
Dennis' Hideaway (£)
One for island hoppers on a budget, Dennis offers comfy rooms with balconies and a warm welcome.
✉ **Mayreau** ☎ **/fax (784) 458-8594**

Young Island (£££)
Private island resort just off shore offering rustic luxury in wood and stone cottages surrounded by tropical greenery. Watersports and yachting activities.
✉ **Opposite Villa, St Vincent** ☎ **(784) 458-4826; fax (784) 457-4567**

All-inclusives and Meal Plans
All-inclusive resort properties are booming in the Caribbean. The one-price package covering transport, board, lodging and activities can be an advantage on the budget organisation front, but all too often the free drinks and entertainment are a poor excuse for bland accommodation, dreary food and little or no contact with the outside world. Always check what type of meal plan your hotel offers. European Plan (EP) does not include any meals; Continental Plan (CP) includes breakfast; Modified American Plan (MAP) guarantees two full meals daily; Full American Plan (FAP) three meals a day.

Western Caribbean

Black Coral and Tortoiseshell

Many visitors will come across black coral jewellery and tortoiseshell items (made from the shell of the hawksbill turtle) in the craft markets of the Caribbean. Don't be tempted to buy as it is illegal to import either into the US, the UK and many other countries under CITES (Convention on International Trade in Endangered Species).

The Bahamas

Duty-free shopping is big business in the Bahamas. Savings of around 25 to 40 per cent on US prices are available on a huge range of imported china, crystal, fashions, jewellery, cosmetics, perfumes and electronic goods. Top shopping centres in Freeport/Grand Bahama include the **International Bazaar** and **Port Lucaya** complexes. On New Providence, Nassau's main shopping district is centred on downtown Bay Street, where the **Straw Market** is a glory hole of local crafts and souvenir items.

Cayman Islands

Grand Cayman is a major free port offering discounts of between 25 and 50 per cent on US prices. The **Anchorage Shopping Center** and **Kirk Freeport Center** are two of George Town's busiest malls, and there are several more on West Bay Road, close to Seven Mile Beach. Local crafts can be found at **Pure Art**, South Church Street, or invest in a little salvaged Spanish treasure from **Artifacts**, Harbour Drive.

Dominican Republic

Amber is a best buy in the Dominican Republic, available from a number of stores in Santo Domingo and the **Museo del Ambar** in Puerta Plata (▶ 40). Dominican cigars are also very popular, and Haitian-style local artwork and woodcarvings. Stallholders expect to bargain, so don't disappoint them and secure yourself a bargain.

Jamaica

Jamaica's home-grown souvenirs include Blue Mountain coffee, rum and rum-based liqueurs, the latest reggae tapes and CDs, and fragrant essential oils, soaps and lotions from the Blue Mountain Aromatics Range. All the main resort areas have craft markets, where 'higgling' (haggling) is the norm for jewellery, carvings, straw goods and other souvenirs. Numerous galleries showcase local artists, such as the **Bougainvillea Gallery** in Negril, and **Harmony Hall**, outside Ocho Rios, which is also renowned for the quality and variety of its Caribbean arts and crafts.

Duty-fee shopping is popular in Montego Bay's City Centre shopping district and the upscale new Half Moon Village in the Rose Hall area. In Ocho Rios, try the Ocean Village Shopping Centre or Soui's Plaza.

Puerto Rico

Puerto Rico is not a duty-free zone, but the island has no sales tax, so in-store prices still represent an attractive saving on US price tags. Old San Juan is a magnet for keen shoppers offering a wide range of fashions, luxury goods and galleries. Well worth a visit is **Puerto Rican Arts & Crafts**, Calle Fortaleza 204, the place to shop for handmade *santos* (pottery figures), *mundillo* (lace), hammocks and carnival masks. Good quality Haitian art is on sale at **The Haitian Gallery**, Calle Fortaleza 367. The Condado hotel district is renowned for its designer boutiques.

Eastern Caribbean

Barbados

Duty-free shopping is well developed in the popular cruise port of Bridgetown. Downtown Broad Street is awash with duty-free outlets, including the **Cave Shepherd** and **Harrisons** department stores. Duty-free shoppers will need to show an immigration slip and purchases will be delivered to the airport, cruise ship or hotel. The colourful **Chattel Village** shopping complexes in Holetown and St Lawrence Gap are a good places to go to buy island fashions, gifts and souvenirs. And check out the well-stocked **Best of Barbados** chain with outlets around the island for local crafts, condiments, greetings cards and books.

French Antilles

Guadeloupe

French luxury goods at mainland prices are the chief attraction of shopping in the French Antilles. Pointe-à-Pitre's main shopping area gathers around rue Frébault, rue Schoelcher and the dockside Centre St Jean Perse, providing a good selection of boutiques, perfumeries and stores selling crystal and china. There is a craft market on La Darse for the popular souvenir T-shirts, woodcarvings, bead jewellery and costume dolls in bright *madras* fabrics.

Martinique

Fort-de-France offers the greatest array of stylish designer boutiques and specialist stores in a grid of streets bounded by rue Victor Hugo, rue de la République, and rue de la Liberté. A favourite purchase in the jewellery line is the *chaîne forçat*, a gold slave chain necklace worn with traditional Creole costume. Other good buys are rum, and crafts from the **Centre des Métiers d'Art**, rue Ernest Deproge.

St-Barthélemy

Duty-free Gustavia has outposts of **Cartier**, **Gucci** and **Hermès** among other illustrious designer names. Perfumes, jewellery and watches are top buys, and wine buffs can contemplate the finest vintages at the **Cellier du Gouverneur**, quai de la République.
Over the hill in St Jean, the Villa Créole Mall has a small selection of boutiques including **La Boutique Made In St-Barth** featuring assorted crafts and souvenir T-shirts which are produced on the island.

St-Martin

Marigot is a fashionable spot with a number of well-known European designers featured in the Marina Port La Royale shopping complex and along rue du Général de Gaulle. There are numerous art galleries, too, including **Gingerbread & Mahogany**, in the marina, one of the most respected Haitian galleries in the region. Local artist Roland Richardson has a gallery on rue de la République. In the seaside village of Grande Case, the **Lynn Studio** on the main street displays colourful island scenes by Gloria and Peter Lynn, another talented local duo.

Duty-free Caution

A word of warning for big spenders planning a major spree in the Caribbean's top duty-free ports: check prices back home before you lash out. In most cases, there are considerable bargains to be had on expensive items such as cameras, hi-fi equipment and jewellery, but a little advance detective work can ensure that a duty-free bargain does not turn into a liability when the import duty bill is presented at the end of the holiday.

Island Art
There are galleries galore in the islands and some very good local artists to look out for. Widely reproduced on everything from postcards and prints to tablewear are Gloria Lynn's jolly market ladies and Donald Dahlke's fishwives. Originals can be found in better galleries. Elsewhere, Kate Spencer captures tropical scenes in the Leeward Islands; Roland Richardson records life on St-Martin; and in St Lucia, look out for works by Xavier Llewellyn and rising young Dominican-born painter Arnold Toulon.

Leeward Islands

Anguilla
For serious shopping, most visitors take the ferry to neighbouring St-Martin/Sint Maarten, but Anguilla has several interesting local galleries. **Cheddie's Carving Studio** is a showcase for talented local sculptor Cheddie Richardson's driftwood carvings. In the Valley, the **Savannah Gallery** carries a wide range of Haitian art and paintings and photographic prints by local artists.

Antigua
Conveniently located by the cruise berth in St John's, the dockside **Heritage Quay** complex contains a number of duty-free stores. **Redcliffe Quay**'s boutiques are a good hunting ground for island fashions and stylish contemporary jewellery from **Goldsmitty**. A short drive from Nelson's Dockyard, check out the prints, pottery and batik clothing crammed into the **Seahorse Studios Art Gallery** at Falmouth Harbour. There is a larger and more varied selection of quality Caribbean art and crafts at **Harmony Hall**, rather off the beaten track on the east coast, but well worth a visit.

St Kitts and Nevis
Downtown Basseterre offers a small but tempting array of galleries and gift shops. On **The Circus**, **Island Hopper** stocks colourful beachwear and Caribbean crafts. **Kate Design**, Bank Street, is a showcase for local artist Kate Spencer's prints, cards, table mats and painted silk clothing, while the **Spencer Cameron Gallery** on Independence Square exhibits work by artists from around the region. The **Caribelle Batik** workshops (▶ 72) are another favourite shopping diversion.
On Nevis, Caribelle's bright tropical designs are also on sale at **Island Hopper** in Charlestown, and Kate Spencer has an outlet here. Keen stamp collectors can also stop in at the **Nevis Philatelic Bureau** near the ferry berth.

Netherlands Antilles

Aruba
A top cruise port, Oranjestad is well supplied with duty-free stores in the **Wharfside Mall** and **Seaport Mall & Marketplace**. Jewellery, watches, china and crystal are good buys and are stocked by **Gandelman Jewelers** at several locations around town. The Tuesday evening **Bom Bini Festival** at Fort Zoutman is a good source of arts and crafts.

Curaçao
Willemstad's major duty-free stores and boutiques are centred around Breedestraat in the Punda district. Delft china, jewellery and electronic goods are all popular buys. Near the cruise-ship berth in Otrobanda, the **Arawak Crafts Products** ceramic factory has an outlet store selling cute pottery replicas of Dutch colonial buildings. Local artists and photographers are represented in the eye-catching **Kas Di Alma Blou** gallery opposite.

Sint Maarten

Philipsburg is one of the top Caribbean duty-free ports offering savings of between 25 and 50 per cent on a huge range of imported luxury goods from around the world. There are particularly good deals to be had on electronic goods, jewellery, watches, linen and leather. Front Street is the heart of the action, and there is a busy crafts market behind the Courthouse on Back Street. If you are after local art, pay a visit to **Greenwith Galleries**, 20 Front Street.

Trinidad & Tobago

Tobago

Tobago's only tourist shopping area is the little **Store Bay** shopping village, a clutch of wooden huts offering colourful batik and tie-dye beachwraps, T-shirts, straw hats, woodcarvings, pottery and other local crafts.

Trinidad

The lower end of Frederick Street in Port of Spain is the best hunting ground for Trinidadian souvenirs. A teeming international bazaar of Indian sari shops and street hustlers, it is the place to stock up on the latest Carnival Road March, calypso and soca CDs, jewellery, leatherwork and kitsch miniature steel pans or Rasta hats with fake dreadlocks.

There is more up-market shopping to be had amongst the chic boutiques and galleries on Nook Avenue, St Anne, and the **Ellerslie Court** shopping centre in Maraval.

Virgin Islands

Tortola (BVI)

For the best selection of island souvenirs in Road Town, stop off at the **Sunny Caribbee Spice Co** on Main Street, and stock up on tropical fruit teas, chutneys, pepper sauces and other tasty gifts. The adjacent art gallery features an interesting selection of paintings, prints, pottery and woodcarvings by Caribbean artists.

St Croix (USVI)

Downtown Christiansted has plenty to offer the keen shopper. The open-air **King's Alley Walk** mall has a good selection of boutiques, gift shops, galleries and crafts stalls. Jewellery stores do a busy trade in souvenir Cruzan Hook bracelets. On Strand Street, **Folk Art Traders** deal in top-quality Caribbean arts and crafts from around the region. A popular stop on a round-island tour is the **St Croix LEAP** woodwork studio on Route 76, north of Frederiksted.

St John (USVI)

The shopping on St John is considered small beer after the mercantile frenzy of St Thomas, but there are several good reasons to stop off at the attractive **Mongoose Junction** shopping complex. **R & I Patton Goldsmithing** create a tempting range of island-inspired jewellery; seek out the hand-painted clothing by local designer Sloop Jones; or get kitted out with hiking gear from **Big Planet Adventurer Outfitters**.

Good News for US Citizens

St Thomas (▶ 108) is a famous Caribbean duty-free enclave, but shoppers from mainland US have an added incentive to bargain hunt in the USVI of St Croix and St John as well. At the end of their holiday they can take full advantage of a generous $1,200 duty-free allowance for purchases made on the islands, and that applies to children, too. However, do keep receipts in case they are required as proof of purchase by US Customs.

Island Spice

Grenada lives up to its name as the Spice Island of the Caribbean. Nutmeg, cinnamon, cloves, allspice and bay rum are all grown on the island and sold by spice ladies gathered at the foot of the cruise-ship gangplank, in markets and from roadside stalls. No rum punch is considered complete without a dusting of nutmeg and even the national flag is adorned with its very own Grenadian nutmeg.

St Thomas (USVI)

Charlotte Amalie's famous duty-free stores which flank Dronningensgade/Main Street are piled high with English china, French crystal, Italian leather, jewellery, perfumes and all the latest electronic gadgetry discounted by 20 to 50 per cent below US prices. Check out the alleyways leading down to the Waterfront Highway for fashions and gifts. This is the place to find colourful, tropical-style resort wear; swimwear from **Just Add Water** on Royal Dane Mall; and the **Mini Mouse House**, a toy store on Trompeter Gade, which has a great stock of tricks, games and other fun stuff to keep children amused. Cruise passengers will find top stores such as **Little Switzerland**, **Bolchands** and **A.H. Riise** also have outlets in the Havensight Mall. Beyond the City, take a trip to Tillet Gardens for crafts studios and galleries in a quiet artisans' village notable for its basking iguanas. A thoroughly touristy stop is the Mountain Top view point and souvenir mall on Crown Mountain Road.

Windward Islands

Dominica

Shopping is generally pretty low-key on Dominica, with the emphasis on crafts. Several small craft shops in Roseau sell Carib basketware, including **Caribana**, 31 Cork Street, which also exhibits work by local artists. For colourful Caribbean souvenirs, try the **Rainforest Shop**, 17 Old Street.

Grenada

Spices are one of the best buys in Grenada. Little baskets of assorted spices make great gifts or souvenirs and are sold practically everywhere on the island (► panel). In St George's, The Carenage has a selection of small gift shops and galleries, or seek out the **Yellow Poui Art Galleries**, on Young Street, which has a fine reputation for local arts and crafts, photography and antique map prints.

St Lucia

Cheap and cheerful souvenirs, beachwear and jewellery are the stock in trade of Castries' waterfront craft market and the covered vendor's market across the street. For more up-market shopping, browse around the boutiques, duty-free stores and galleries at the **Pointe Seraphine** cruise complex. **Bagshaw Studios** have an outlet here for their tropical print clothing and tableware, or pay a visit to the factory shop at **La Toc**.

St Vincent and the Grenadines

In Kingstown, a small selection of Caribbean souvenirs, beachwear and spices can be found at **Noah's Arkade**, Bay Street, which also has an outpost at the Frangipani Hotel on Bequia. Bequia's waterfront crafts market offers an assortment of beachwear, T-shirts and bead jewellery. Or try the **Local Color** boutique, which combines casual island fashions with cards, prints, souvenirs and silver jewellery.

Children's Attractions

Western Caribbean

Bahamas
Adastra Gardens and Zoo
Animals and birds from Madagascan lemurs to South American monkeys and toothsome caimans to chatty parrots. Visitors can pet tame Bahamian boa constrictors or just sit back and watch the Marching Flamingo show (► 35).
✉ Chippingham Road, Nassau, New Providence ☎ (242) 323-5806 ⏰ Daily 9–5

Puerto Rico
San Felipe del Morro
This Spanish fortress (► 25) is a good place for children to let off steam. There's plenty to explore from the maze of tunnels, ramps and dungeons to the battlement views.
✉ Punta del Morro, San Juan ☎ (787) 729-6960 ⏰ Daily 9:15–5

Eastern Caribbean

Barbados
Barbados Wildlife Reserve (► 56)

French Antilles
Aquarium de la Guadeloupe
The full spectrum of Caribbean marine life gets an outing at this sizeable aquarium, with tiny brightly coloured reef fish, seahorses and cruising black-tipped, nurse and grey sharks. Divers give demonstrations in the main tank and there is a mangrove area reconstruction.
✉ place Créole-Marina, Bas du Fort, Grande-Terre, Guadeloupe ☎ (590) 90-92-38 ⏰ Daily 9–7

Leeward Islands
Caribbean Cove Amusement Park
There is a piratical theme to this small water park with its bumper boats, mini-golf course and games arcade. Bar and live entertainment.
✉ Stoney Ground, Charlestown, Nevis ☎ (869) 469-1286 ⏰ Mon–Fri 10–10, Sat 10–12, Sun 5PM–11PM (Wed–Sun only from mid-May to Oct)

Netherlands Antilles
Curaçao Sea Aquarium
Sea lion and shark pools, tropical fish, sinister eels and touch tanks make this an interesting stop. There is also an Animal Encounters programme (reservations) for snorkellers and divers in a natural reef pool. Sharks can be fed through holes in a plexiglass barrier.
✉ Bapor Kibra, Curaçao ☎ (5999) 461-6666 ⏰ Daily 8:30–6

Trinidad & Tobago
Emperor Valley Zoo
An old-fashioned zoo with a good selection of native and South American animals and birds including tapirs, capybaras, porcupines and a giant Brazilian otter measuring around 6ft (2m).
✉ Queen's Park Savannah North Side, Port of Spain, Trinidad ☎ (868) 622-3530 ⏰ Daily 9:30–6

US Virgin Islands
Coral World
This marine park's 80,000-gallon (363,680-litre) reef tank, 21 aquariums, turtle, stingray, baby shark and touch pools provide plenty to see and do. Also daily talks and fish-feeding sessions.
✉ Coki Point, St Thomas ☎ (340) 775-1555 ⏰ Daily 9–5:30

Let the Hotel Help
Family-style attractions are in short supply in the Caribbean, so parents are strongly advised to select their accommodation with a view to keeping the kids entertained. Most hotels in the family market offer a range of supervised children's activity programmes, but while watersports and tennis may keep older children occupied, parents of younger children should find out whether the hotel offers programmes suited to their child's age group and interests.

Activities

Good Reasons for a Guide

Hiking is becoming increasingly popular in the Caribbean islands, but with very few exceptions most rainforest trails are unmarked and it is easy to get well and truly lost. Rainy season mudslides and fast-growing tropical foliage can only add to the confusion. The best way to navigate the forest is with an experienced guide. Their fund of local knowledge will also add considerably to the experience.

Day Sails

St Lucia

A day sail is a great way for holidaymakers staying in the Rodney Bay/Castries area to see the famous Pitons and the sights around Soufrière.

Brig Unicorn ☎ **(758) 452-6811; Endless Summer** ☎ **(758) 450-8651; M/Y Vigie** ☎ **(758) 452-3762**

St Vincent

Set sail around the island to visit the Falls of Baleine, or head off down the Grenadines on a day-sail excursion with a picnic lunch and snorkelling gear.

Baleine Tours ☎ **(784) 457-4089; Fantasea Tours** ☎ **(784) 457-4477**

Tortola (BVI)

Visitors can explore the marvellous vistas, uninhabited islands and hidden beach coves of Drake's Passage on a day sail with lunch and snorkelling.

Patouche II ☎ **(284) 494-6300; Silmaril** ☎ **(284) 495-9225**

Golf

St Croix (USVI)

The Robert Trent Jones-designed championship course at the Carambola Golf Club is set in the gently rolling hills in the northwest of the island.

✉ **Davis Bay** ☎ **(340) 778-5638**

St Thomas (USVI)

One of the Caribbean's most scenic golfing experiences is on the challenging Mahogany Run course.

✉ **Mahogany Run Road** ☎ **(340) 775-7050; reservations** ☎ **(340) 777-6006**

Hiking and Eco-Tours

Dominica

The top hike in the Morne Trois Pitons National Park is a challenging 7–8 hour round-trip to the steaming volcanic Boiling Lake. Ken's Hinterland Adventures lead guided hikes in the park and birdwatching tours in the Northern Forest Reserve.

✉ **Roseau** ☎ **(767) 448-4850**

Dominican Republic

The Dominican Republic's five national parks range from areas of unspoilt rainforest to coastal mangrove swamplands. Hikers and birdwatchers need permission to access the parks. For information and to arrange a guide, contact the Dirección Nacional de Parques.

✉ **Avenida Independencia 359, Santo Domingo** ☎ **(809) 221-5340**

Grenada

The Grand Etang National Park (▶ 18–19) in Grenada's central highlands offers a range of short walks from the park centre and more challenging rainforest hikes (best undertaken with a local guide) to the summit of Mt Qua Qua, the Concord Valley and waterfall beauty spots.

Henry's Safari Tours ☎ **(473) 444-5313; Telfor Hiking Tours** ☎ **(473) 442-6200**

Guadeloupe (▶ 24)

Jamaica
Black River Safaris
Regular safari boat rides explore the Great Morass, a mangrove swamp area on

Jamaica's south coast, teeming with undisturbed wildlife from herons and egrets to basking crocodiles.
✉ **Black River** 🕒 **Schedules and information, contact South Coast Safaris** ☎ **(876) 965-2513**

Puerto Rico
Several local adventure and eco-tourism operators offer a variety of activities such as caving, kayaking, mountain-biking, birdwatching and rainforest hikes, as well as trips to plantations and other sites of historical and natural interest.
Copladet Nature & Adventure Travel ☎ **(787) 765-8595; Ecanto Ecotours** ☎ **(787) 272-0005; Tropix Wellness Tours** ☎ **(787) 268-2173**

St John, USVI (▶ 25)

St Lucia
There are several excellent hikes and birdwatching opportunities in the 19,000-acre (76,890ha) National Rainforest, accessible from Fonds St Jacques (above Soufrière), and the Barre de L'Isle Trail (east of Castries). Permission must be obtained from the Forestry Department in advance, who also provide guides.
Forestry Department ☎ **(758) 450-2331 or 2086**

St Vincent
For a sighting of the rare St Vincent parrot, try the Parrot Lookout on the well-marked Vermont Nature Trails leading up from the Buccament Valley. Or take a hike up to the crater rim of La Soufrière. Local operators offer guided rainforest and volcano hikes, bird-watching and trips to local beauty spots such as Trinity Falls.
HazeECO Tours ☎ **(784) 457-8634; SVG Tours** ☎ **(784) 458-4534**

Horse-riding

Antigua
There are some good riding trails through the hilly terrain behind the southeast coast and fine views from upland spots.
Spring Hill Riding Club ✉ **Falmouth Harbour** ☎ **(268) 463-8041; St James's Club** ✉ **Mamora Bay** ☎ **(268) 460-5000**

Aruba
Saddle up for a trail across the cactus-dotted and desert-like cunucu landscape.
Rancho del Campo ☎ **(297) 820290; Rancho El Paso** ☎ **(297) 873310**

Sportfishing

Cayman Islands
Deep-sea fishing comes second only to diving among Grand Cayman's sporting attractions. Blue and white marlin, sailfish and bonefish are among the enticements.
Charter Boat Headquarters ✉ **Coconut Shopping Plaza** ☎ **(345) 945-4340**

St Thomas (USVI)
Several sportfishing outfits operate from the American Yacht Harbour at Red Hook in the East End. Expect dolphinfish, kingfish and wahoo, also blue marlin in spring (Mar–Jun).
Prowler Sportfishing Charters Inc ☎ **(340) 779-5939; St Thomas Fishing Center** ☎ **(340) 775-7990**

Dolphin Encounters
Schools of wild bottlenose and spinner dolphins are regularly spotted off the Virgin Islands, Windward Islands and the Bahamas. In Grand Bahama several companies offer popular dolphin encounter programmes which enable participants to observe or swim and dive with dolphins. Make reservations well in advance with Dolphin Experience ☎ (242) 373-1250 or UNEXSO ☎ (242) 373-1244.

Diving

Dive Packages
Hotel dive packages are an increasingly popular option for keen divers and active holidaymakers looking to learn, and are widely available throughout the Caribbean. Packages cater for both beginners and experienced divers, and many also offer refresher courses for qualified divers who have not taken the plunge recently. Accommodation can be selected to suit your budget, from simple dive lodges to top-of-the-range hotels.

Western Caribbean

Bahamas
Excellent reef and wreck diving with a good chance of spotting sharks and dolphins. Trips can also be arranged to the outer islands such as Andros close to the third largest barrier reef in the world.
UNEXSO ✉ **Grand Bahama** ☎ **(242) 373-1244; Dive Dive Dive, New Providence** ☎ **(242) 362-1142; Small Hope Bay Lodge** ✉ **Andros** ☎ **(242) 368 2014**

Cayman Islands
Top diving destination famous for its spectacular 'walls', near-vertical drops plummeting to 6,000ft (1,830m) within a mile of the shore, clustered with corals and inhabited by a staggering variety of marine life.
Bob Soto's Diving Ltd, Grand Cayman ☎ **(345) 949-2022; Don Foster's Dive Cayman, Grand Cayman** ☎ **(345) 945-5132); Peter Hughes Dive Tiara, Cayman Brac and Little Cayman** ☎ **(345) 948-1553**

Eastern Caribbean

Anguilla
Anguilla has six marine parks and seven wreck dives, including Spanish galleons and more recent artificial reef sites which have attracted schooling fish. There is superb snorkelling in the shallows.
Anguilla Divers Ltd ☎ **(264) 497-4750; Dive Shop Anguilla** ☎ **(264) 497-2020**

Bonaire
The Bonaire Marine Park is world-renowned (▶ 17, Top Ten). The best diving is off the sheltered west coast.
Captain Don's Habitat Dive Center ☎ **(5997) 8290; Dive Bonaire** ☎ **(5997) 8285; Sand Dollar Dive and Photo** ☎ **(5997) 5252**

Curaçao
Several of Curaçao's 100-plus sheltered reef dive sites compare favourably with neighbouring Bonaire. Superb visibility and diverse marine life. The more challenging sites are in the northern Banda Abao Underwater Park.
Habitat Curaçao ☎ **(5999) 464-8800; Underwater Curaçao** ☎ **(5999) 461-8100**

Dominica
Quietly emerging as one of the best dive destinations in the region, the Scotts Head/Soufrière Bay Marine Park encompasses a volcanic crater fringed by pinnacles and reefs teeming with fish, turtles and rays. A further clutch of dive sites lie off the Cabrits National Park.
Cabrits Dive Centre ☎ **(767) 445-3010; Dive Dominica** ☎ **(767) 448-2188; Nature Island Dive** ☎ **(767) 449-8181**

Grenada
Good sites for beginners and experienced divers in the Molinere Point area just north of St George's. The most exciting dives are the 600ft (180m) *Bianca C* cruise-ship wreck and the Kick 'em Jenny submarine volcano.
Dive Grenada ☎ **(473) 444-1092; Grand Anse Aquatics** ☎ **(473) 444-1046**

Martinique
In St Pierre harbour, wrecks dating from the 1902

eruption of Mont Pelée make interesting diving. Martinique's best coral reef sites are off the south coast. **L'Ile Bleue** ☎ (596) 66-06-90; **Sub Diamond Rock** ☎ (596) 76-25-80; **Tropicasub St Pierre** ☎ (596) 78-38-03

Saba

Tiny Saba offers mega-diving in the pristine depths of the Saba Marine Park (▶ panel opposite). **Saba Deep Dive** ☎ (5994) 63347; **Saba Reef Divers** ☎ (5994) 62541

St Croix (USVI)

A fringe of coral reefs and a fine wall drop-off parallel to the northwest coast, accessible from Salt River and from the shore at Cane Bay. There are also several good sites around Frederiksted. **Anchor Dive Center** ☎ (340) 778-1522; **Cane Bay Dive Shop** ☎ (340) 773-9913

St Lucia

Plummeting drop-offs in the Soufrière Marine Park mirror St Lucia's dramatic terrestrial terrain, and a combination of pristine corals, myriad marine life and good visibility make this a top Caribbean dive destination ideal for beginners and experienced . **Rosemond's Trench Divers** ☎ (758) 451-4761; **Scuba St Lucia** ☎ (758) 459-7755

St Thomas (USVI)

Calm water, good visibility and easy access to reef sites around the uninhabited offshore cays make St Thomas a good bet for beginners. A smattering of wrecks also exists for more experienced divers, and local

operators arrange trips to the RMS *Rhone* in the BVI (see below). **Chris Sawyer Diving Center** ☎ (340) 777-7804; **Coki Beach Dive & Snorkel Center** ☎ (340) 775-6100

St Vincent & the Grenadines

Good coral reef diving off St Vincent can be combined with excursions to the Grenadines, notably the HMS *Purina* wreck site off Mayreau, and gorgeous Tobago Cays. Individual dive trips and ten-dive, island-hopper packages are available through the following operators. **Dive St Vincent** ☎ (784) 457-4928; **Dive Bequia** ☎ (784) 458-3504; **Dive Canouan** ☎ (784) 458-8044; **Grenadines Dive (Union Island)** ☎ (784) 458-8122

Tortola & Virgin Gorda (BVI)

Well-populated reefs and pinnacles, plus a whole host of wreck dives provide great diving in the BVI. The most famous wreck is the RMS *Rhone*, sunk off the coast of Salt Island in 1867. **Blue Water Divers, Tortola** ☎ (284) 494-2847; **Dive BVI, Virgin Gorda** ☎ (284) 495-5513

Tobago

Fabulous diving off the north coast of the island where a colony of giant manta rays (nicknamed 'Tobago taxis') and sightings of dolphins, hammerhead sharks and whale sharks add to the spectacular underwater scenery. **Aqua Marine Dive** ☎ (868) 639-4416; **Man Friday Diving** ☎ (868) 660-4676

Spectacular Saba

Saba's dramatically rugged underwater landscape is a complex tapestry of brilliant coral gardens, huge volcanic boulders carpeted in sponges, dizzying drop-offs and towering pinnacles which act as a magnet for rays, groupers, schools of silver jacks and larger fish. The submarine walls plummet down 1,000ft (305m) within half-a-mile of the shore, and in the calm of winter visibility can reach upwards of 125ft (38m).

Nightlife

Live Music

Reggae, steel pan, calypso and jazz – live music is a moveable feast in the islands but there is never any shortage. Where you'll find the live bands often depends which night of the week it is, so ask around or just follow the crowd (and your ears). There is rarely an admission charge in bars, where most of the local bands play, and most hotels welcome non-residents. Dancing is impromptu, but most people do it, so let your hair down and enjoy.

Western Caribbean

Bahamas

The King and Knights Club
King Eric and his remarkably agile knights take to the stage for an action-packed display of limbo and fire-dancing accompanied by steel drums, Bahamian music and song.

✉ **Nassau Beach Hotel, Nassau, New Providence** ☎ **(242) 327-771** ⊙ **Tue–Sat 8:30PM and 10:30PM, Sun–Mon 8:30PM only**

Paradise Island Casino and Atlantis Showroom
These two night spots are side by side. You can take in a Caribbean dinner show at the Atlantis Showroom and then gamble the night away at the casino.

✉ **Atlantis Paradise Island Resort, Nassau, New Providence** ☎ **Reservations (242) 363-3000** ⊙ **Nightly**

Cayman Islands

Coconuts Comedy Club and Barefoot Man & Band
Two of the island's most popular after-dark entertainment venues can be found in one hotel. Regular comedy evenings are held in the English-style pub, while Barefoot Man provides live music in the friendly beach bar.

✉ **Hyatt Regency Grand Cayman, Seven Mile Beach, Grand Cayman** ☎ **(345) 945-4444** ⊙ **Barefoot Man, nightly; Coconuts, check schedules**

Jamaica

Tino's Reggae Café
A continuation of MoBay's Gloucester Avenue bar, dining and entertainment-packed 'Hip Strip', the outdoor action at Tino's is audible before it is visible.

✉ **Cornwall Beach, Montego Bay** ⊙ **Nightly**

Hotel SamSara
The place to catch live shows by the best local reggae bands (regular concerts Mon) and visiting overseas artists (check schedules). There is also a sports bar and discothèque.

✉ **Light House Road, Negril** ☎ **(876) 957-4395** ⊙ **Nightly**

Renaissance Jamaica Grande
A whole host of live entertainment options for night owls. Jump-Up Carnival parties, music showcases, nightclubs and the hugely popular Jamaic'N Me Crazy discothèque.

✉ **Main Street, Ocho Rios** ☎ **(876) 974-2201** ⊙ **Nightly**

Puerto Rico

Condado Plaza Hotel & Casino
Multi-faceted night-time venue boasting the largest casino on the island, the Copa Room nightclub, La Fiesta showroom for Latino spectaculars and Isadora's discothèque.

✉ **999 Ashford Avenue, Condado, San Juan** ☎ **(787) 721-1000** ⊙ **Nightly**

LeLoLai Festival
Part of the LeLoLai cultural programme, folkloric shows showcasing Puerto Rican country music and dancing and flamenco are staged at several hotels in San Juan each week. Call for information and reservations.

✉ **Puerto Rico Tourism Co (LeLoLai Division), San Juan** ☎ **(787) 723-3132**

Eastern Caribbean

Barbados
1627 and all that...
This entertaining folkloric show traces the island's history through Bajan song and dance accompanied by African drums and steel band music in a suitably historic setting.

✉ **Barbados Museum, Garrison Savannah** ☏ **(246) 428-1627** 🕐 **Thu and Sun**

French Antilles
Zoo Rock Café
One of around two dozen or so happening music bars and discos in the Bas du Fort/Gosier area. The Zoo Rock Café attracts a hip crowd and offers cocktails and both live and DJ music. Join them and then just follow the crowd on to the next lively venue.

✉ **Marina Bas du Fort, Grande-Terre, Guadeloupe** ☏ **(590) 90-77-77** 🕐 **Nightly**

Leeward Islands
The Mainbrace
Packed full of yachties, tourists and local lads, the Mainbrace is a pub-style bar serving 'twofers' (two for one drinks) on Tuesday and Friday nights. Music and dancing.

✉ **Copper & Lumber Store, Nelson's Dockyard, English Harbour, Antigua**
☏ **(268) 463-1058**
🕐 **Nightly**

Mango's
Pleasant restaurant that turns into the hottest spot on the island on Friday nights, when the courtyard bar is packed and the music plays loud and late.

✉ **Independence Square,**

Basseterre, St Kitts
☏ **(869) 465-4049**
🕐 **Closed Sun**

Netherlands Antilles
Landhuis Brievengat
This pretty Dutch Colonial estate house is decked out with fairy lights and tables on the terrace for weekly dinner dances (Friday), and special evening folkloric shows on the first Sunday of the month (reservations are necessary).

✉ **Brievengat, Curaçao**
☏ **(5999) 737-8344**

Maho Beach Hotel & Casino
Gambling is a popular evening activity on Sint Maarten and there are several casinos on Philipsburg's Front Street as well as at this large beach resort. The Maho also has a popular nightclub.

✉ **Maho Bay, Sint Maarten**
☏ **(5995) 52115**
🕐 **Nightly**

US Virgin Islands
Barnacle Bill's
Barnacle Bill's, one of several lively bars in the Sub Base area west of Charlotte Amalie, is a good place to catch live bands and a riotous talent night on Monday.

✉ **Submarine Base, St Thomas**
☏ **(340) 774-7444** 🕐 **Nightly**

Windward Islands
Gros Islet Jump-Up
Visitors and locals hit the street in Gros Islet for a fun night of dancing to reggae, soca and French Caribbean zouk music, fuelled by handy barbecue stalls.

✉ **Rodney Bay, St Lucia**
🕐 **Fri**

Caribbean Theme Nights
Many larger hotels feature a Caribbean evening as part of their weekly events itinerary. The usual form is cocktails and a West Indian buffet accompanied by steel pan music, followed by singers, dancers and acrobats performing a varied menu of limbo-dancing, fire-eating, walking on broken bottles and other feats. The evening winds up with a chance to dance under the stars.

What's On When

Carnival Timetable

Preparations for a Caribbean Carnival begin almost as soon as the previous year's festivities are over. Rehearsals and preliminary competitions for the pre-Lent carnivals start soon after Christmas and run up to the Friday before Lent when Carnival kicks off in earnest with a weekend of costume and calypso competitions, music and dancing. Monday's celebrations begin with the pre-dawn Jouvert jump-up and continue right through the day. The main procession and carnival band finals are traditionally held on Shrove Tuesday or Mardi Gras.

January

Three King's Day, Puerto Rico: island-wide fiestas with parades, music and dance to celebrate Epiphany (6 Jan).

February

Reggae Sunsplash, Jamaica: huge crowds gather in Ocho Rios for this major reggae music fest. (Also ► Carnival, below.)

March

Carnival: many Caribbean islands celebrate Carnival in the run-up to Lent (Feb–Mar), culminating on Shrove Tuesday. The most famous is the spectacular Trinidad Carnival in Port of Spain.

April

Sailing Week, Antigua: yachties gather for fun regattas, serious racing and non-stop partying at the end of the sailing season.

May

St Lucia International Jazz Festival, St Lucia: top-flight musicians and fans jet in for this world-class four-day festival.

June

Million Dollar Month, Cayman Islands: a month-long sportfishing extravaganza promising big fish and big prizes.
St Kitts Music Festival, St Kitts: a relatively new but hot musical event attracting an international line-up of reggae, calypso, jazz and gospel acts.

July

Fourth of July, St John (USVI): St John's Carnival Parade dovetails neatly with US Independence Day celebrations.
Crop Over, Barbados: marking the end of the sugar harvest, this five-week festival combines arts, crafts, music and local events culminating in a huge carnival parade (first Mon of Aug).

August

Fête des Cuisinières, Guadeloupe: gastronomic showcase for female chefs with colourful parades, traditional costumes, cook-offs and terrific Creole food in Pointe-à-Pitre.

September

Gone fishing: the quietest month of the low season with no major events, but the fishing is good...

October

Pirates Week Festival, Cayman Islands: plenty of rum, street parades, fancy dress competitions and musical and sporting events.

November

World Zouk-Cadence Festival, Dominica: Dominica celebrates the Creole rhythms of the French Caribbean as part of the island's Independence Day celebrations (3 Nov).

December

Junkanoo, Bahamas: Bahamian carnival hits the streets with elaborate costume parades, stilt-riding mocko jumbies (spirit figures), music, dance and mayhem (26 Dec–Jan).
Foxy's New Year's Party, Jost van Dyke (BVI): several thousand revellers endeavour to find their way to this notorious beach party (► 80).

Practical Matters

Above: *Marigot's Gingerbread Express ferry,*
St Lucia
Right: *laundry day, Dominican Republic*

117

TIME DIFFERENCES: WESTERN CARIBBEAN

GMT	Western Caribbean	Germany	USA (NY)	Netherlands	Spain
12 noon	← 7AM	→ 1PM	← 7AM	→ 1PM	→ 1PM

BEFORE YOU GO

WHAT YOU NEED

Documentation

A valid passport and an onward or return ticket are sufficient for entry to most Caribbean islands. However, visitors to the Dominican Republic from the UK, US, Canada, France, Germany, Holland and several other countries will have to purchase a US$10 'tourist card' on arrival. In many places US and Canadian citizens need only provide proof of identity in the form of a driver's licence or voter registration card, but always check with your travel agent before setting off. Local immigration forms (distributed by the airline) should also be completed and will be collected on arrival. Non-US visitors to the US Virgin Islands and Puerto Rico have to comply with US immigration requirements. British passport holders and other nationals participating in the US Visa Waiver programme will need to submit a completed visa waiver form (available from the airline check-in) on arrival. The accommodation section of this form must be completed, or entry may be refused.

Cruise-ship passengers will complete immigration formalities on board before being allowed ashore.

Inoculations and Health Precautions

No inoculations or vaccinations are required but immunisation against polio and tetanus is recommended. Visitors to the Dominican Republic may also want to consider protection against malaria. AIDS is present throughout the region.

WHEN TO GO

Kingston, Jamaica

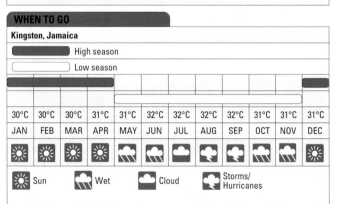

| High season |
| Low season |

30°C	30°C	30°C	31°C	31°C	32°C	32°C	32°C	32°C	31°C	31°C	31°C
JAN	FEB	MAR	APR	MAY	JUN	JUL	AUG	SEP	OCT	NOV	DEC
☀	☀	☀	☀	🌧	🌧	🌩	🌩	🌩	🌧	🌧	☀

☀ Sun   🌧 Wet   ☁ Cloud   🌩 Storms/Hurricanes

The Caribbean region lies in the tropics, so temperatures are fairly consistent year-round and the heat is generally tempered by cooling trade winds. Temperatures average 16–30°C during the day and 15–18°C at night. The driest time of year (and the most popular with visitors) is between December and April; the wettest months are May/June and October/November. In recent years, several newsworthy hurricanes have swept through the region, causing considerable damage in the northeastern Caribbean and the Greater Antilles. The official hurricane season runs from June to October, but a hurricane is most likely to occur during the August/September low season.

GMT	Eastern Caribbean	Germany	USA (NY)	Netherlands	Spain
12 noon	8AM	1PM	7AM	1PM	1PM

WHEN YOU ARE THERE

ARRIVING

Beyond immigration control, most Caribbean airports have a tourist information desk providing hotel and public transport details. If there is no hotel shuttle, taxis are often the sole onward transport option, but they are plentiful, and the information desk can supply fare information. On many islands, details of fixed-price fares between the airport and major hotels or tourist areas are posted in the arrivals hall or near the taxi rank.

MONEY

The US dollar is local currency in Puerto Rico, the US and British Virgin Islands, and is accepted with alacrity throughout the region, though change will probably be given in local currency. When restaurant, hotel or taxi prices are given in dollars always check which currency is being quoted – mistakes can be expensive.

US dollar travellers' cheques are widely accepted in hotels, good restaurants and tourist shops, as are major credit cards. There are banks on all the islands, and they do generally offer the best exchange rates, but banking hours vary, service can be slow and few banks offer ATM cashpoint facilities.

• **Bahamas** Bahamian dollar (B$), fixed at par and interchangeable with the US dollar.
• **Barbados** Barbados dollar (Bds$), fixed against the US dollar.
• **Cayman Islands** Cayman Islands dollar (CI$), fixed against the US dollar.
• **Dominican Republic** Dominican peso (RD$), floats against other currencies. Only buy a few pesos as they are difficult to convert back to foreign currency.
• **French Antilles** French franc (Fr), though US dollars are accepted in tourist areas.
• **Leeward and Windward Islands** Eastern Caribbean dollar (EC$), fixed against the US dollar.
• **Jamaica** Jamaican dollar (J$), floats against other currencies.
• **Netherlands Antilles and Aruba** The Netherlands Antilles florin (Nafl) and Aruba florin (Af), fixed against the US dollar.
• **Puerto Rico** The US dollar.
• **Virgin Islands** The US dollar in both USVI and BVI.
• **Trinidad and Tobago** Trinidad and Tobago dollar (TT$) floats against other currencies.

TIME

The islands of the Eastern Caribbean, the Dominican Republic and Puerto Rico keep Atlantic Standard Time (GMT–4) year-round, which is one hour ahead of US Eastern Standard Time. The Bahamas, Cayman Islands, Jamaica and other islands in the Western Caribbean keep Eastern Standard Time (GMT–5) year-round. Daylight Saving is not observed in the region, so calculate the time difference accordingly.

CUSTOMS

Arriving
The amount travellers can bring in varies from island to island. As a rule, the limit stands at a quart (approximately one litre) of wine or spirits and 200 cigarettes for every adult (aged over 18).

Departing
US citizens, in addition to their duty-free allowance of $1,200 on goods purchased in the USVI, can also take home a further $1,000-worth of goods at five per cent import tax, and pay no duty on items manufactured in the USVI (► 104–108 for other duty-free information).

WHEN YOU ARE THERE

EMERGENCY NUMBERS

The emergency telephone numbers listed below will connect callers with the islands' emergency services or directly to the local police.

Western Caribbean
Bahamas ☎ 919
Cayman Islands ☎ 911
Dominican Republic 711
Jamaica ☎ 119
Puerto Rico ☎ 911

Eastern Caribbean
Barbados ☎ 112

French Antilles
Guadeloupe ☎ 117
Martinique ☎ 117
St Barthélemy ☎ 117
St-Martin ☎ 87-50-04

Leeward Islands
Anguilla ☎ 911
Antigua ☎ 462-0125/8
St Kitts ☎ 469-2241
Nevis ☎ 469-5391

Netherlands Antilles
Aruba ☎ 115
Bonaire ☎ 113 or 2000
Curaçao ☎ 114
Saba:
  The Bottom ☎ 63237
  The Windwardside ☎ 62221
Sint Eustatius ☎ 82333
Sint Maarten ☎ 22222

Trinidad & Tobago ☎ 999

Virgin Islands
B.V.I. ☎ 999
U.S.V.I. ☎ 119

Windward Islands
Dominica ☎ 999
Grenada ☎ 911
St Lucia ☎ 911
St Vincent ☎ 457-1211

NATIONAL HOLIDAYS

1 Jan	New Year's Day
Mar/Apr	Easter
25 Dec	Christmas Day
26 Dec	Boxing Day

The dates of other national holidays, such as Carnival and annual Independence Day celebrations, vary from island to island. Information is available from the tourist office and local hotels.

OPENING HOURS

○ Shops	● Attractions/museums
● Offices	○ Post offices
● Banks	○ Pharmacies

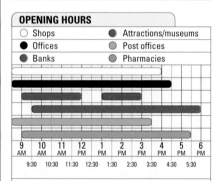

9 AM	10 AM	11 AM	12 PM	1 PM	2 PM	3 PM	4 PM	5 PM	6 PM
9:30	10:30	11:30	12:30	1:30	2:30	3:30	4:30	5:30	

Caribbean opening hours are very flexible, and occasionally frustrating for visitors. In main towns and tourist areas, offices are generally open Monday to Friday 8/8:30–4/4:30 with a lunchtime break. Banking hours are approximately Monday to Friday 9–noon and 1–3, though some may open longer on Fridays. Post offices are open Monday to Friday 8–3:30, Friday until 4:30, and possibly Saturday morning. Shops are open Monday to Friday 8–4, with a lunch break, and Saturday 8–1. However, tourist shops in resort areas, and duty-free stores at cruise-ship destinations, may open later in the day, stay open longer and do business on Saturday afternoons and Sundays. They may also close off-season. Sightseeing attractions are often a law unto themselves. Smaller, less visited sights may not bother to open if business looks slow in the off-season, despite the hours posted at the entrance or in tourist literature.

Bahamas
Barbados
Cayman Islands
Leeward Islands
Jamaica
DRIVE ON THE **Trinidad & Tobago**
LEFT **Virgin Islands (USVI & BVI)**
Windward Islands

Dominican Republic
French Antilles
Puerto Rico

DRIVE ON THE
RIGHT

PUBLIC TRANSPORT

Air The Caribbean is well served by regular short-hop air services linking even the smallest island with its neighbours on a daily basis. Antigua, Barbados, Puerto Rico, St Thomas and Sint Maarten are among the chief regional transport hubs. Major local carriers include Puerto Rico-based American Eagle, and LIAT, which has the Eastern Caribbean comprehensively covered as far west as Puerto Rico. Numerous smaller operations cover a variety of routes offering plenty of choice for travellers.

Sea Regular and inexpensive ferry services ply several routes between the US Virgin Islands of St Thomas and St John, and the neighbouring British Virgin Islands. In the Leeward Island group, there are regular ferry services between St Kitts and Nevis; frequent daily ferries between Anguilla and St-Martin; and boat trips from St-Martin/Sint Maarten to St-Barthélemy and Saba. In the Windward Island chain, regular high-speed catamaran services link Guadeloupe, Dominica, Martinique and St Lucia. There are several services daily between St Vincent and Bequia, and mailboat services make three trips a week up and down the Grenadines.

Buses Public bus transport is cheap but often chaotic and aimed at early morning and evening commuters. Privately operated minibuses are a much better way to get around. They make regular departures (when the bus is full) from town centres to various destinations around the island. Fares are inexpensive. Let the driver know you want to get out by shouting 'Driver, stop!' and/or rapping on the roof.

TAXIS

There are taxi ranks at airports, cruise-ship berths and in downtown areas. Taxis can also be arranged by your hotel. For straightforward journeys rates are fixed and posted at the airport and tourist office in local currency and US dollars. If you would like to take a half- or full-day tour, the hotel or tourist office will be able to suggest a fair price and may recommend a driver who is also a good guide. Before setting off on any journey, always agree the price with the driver.

DRIVING

Some islands drive on the right, some on the left, but most islanders seem blissfully unaware that it makes any difference. The best advice is to drive defensively. Fortunately, nobody drives very fast in the Caribbean as roads tend to be pretty rough with some truly impressive pot-holes in places. Drivers are liable to stop for a chat on blind corners, goats and other livestock graze on the verges and wander into the road without warning, and children are apt to shoot out from the kerb in pursuit of footballs, cricket balls or each other.

CAR RENTAL

Rental cars are relatively expensive in the Caribbean and it is well worth shopping around. Local rental companies generally offer more competitive rates, but this is often reflected in minimal insurance coverage. Check the excess (which may well be US$1,000 or more) carefully. Cars are rarely offered in pristine condition, so take a careful inventory of existing marks and scratches to avoid paying for them when you return the car. A short test drive around the parking lot is not a bad idea either. Make sure the spare tyre is present (and inflated) and that you have a number to call in the event of a breakdown. Child seats are not required by law, so are rarely available. There are few fuel stations outside main settlements, so always fill up before leaving town.

PERSONAL SAFETY

Violent crime, particularly against tourists, is a rarity in the smaller islands. In more developed areas, such as Jamaica, St Thomas and Trinidad, avoid unlit backstreets and the beach after dark, and do not wander too far off the tourist track without a trustworthy guide.

Petty theft is a universal problem, so keep a close grip on wallets, handbags and cameras. Do not flash large amounts of cash in public, and use the hotel safe for valuables. Lock rental cars and place anything you leave behind in the boot.

When leaving your hotel room, be sure to secure all doors, particularly French windows leading out onto patios or low balconies. Contrary to popular belief, drug laws do exist in the Caribbean, and justice is administered swiftly and severely to anyone arrested in possession of drugs. Smugglers will find their stay uncomfortably extended in a local gaol.

TELEPHONES

The Caribbean telephone system is generally efficient and easy to use, and local calls from public telephones are inexpensive. Public telephones are plentiful and accept local coins. There is also an increasing number of card phones in tourist areas. Pre-paid telephone cards can be purchased from tourist information kiosks, post offices and some shops. The mark-up on calls made from hotel rooms is outrageously high, so use pay phones in the lobby wherever possible. Remember that even though another island may be just a few miles away as the crow flies, island-to-island calls (except islands with the same area code) are international.

International Dialling Codes:

France:	33
Germany:	49
Netherlands:	34
Spain:	34
UK:	44
US:	1

POST

Postage stamps can be purchased from most postcard sellers and the hotel front desk, who will also post any mail, which saves a trip to the post office in town. Inter-island mail services are slow; international post is even slower, so it is common to arrive home several weeks before the postcards turn up. However, stamp collectors are always keen to receive the unusual and colourful stamps produced around the region.

ELECTRICITY

The power supply on most islands is 110 volts AC (60 cycles), similar to the US, though the Windward Islands and French Antilles operate on 220 volts AC (50 cycles), while others use both. Always check with the hotel before plugging in electrical equipment.

TIPS/GRATUITIES

Yes ✓ No ✗		
Restaurants	✓	10–15%
Tour Guides (discretionary)	✓	
Bar Service (discretionary)	✓	
Taxis	✓	10–15%
Porters (per bag)	✓	US$1
Chambermaids	✓	US$1
Hairdressers	✓	10–15%
Toilets	✗	

What to photograph: the Caribbean is ablaze with colourful images from flowers and birdlife to brightly painted fishing boats and bustling market scenes. However, do remember that local people may not prove willing background scenery; ask before you snap.
When to photograph: avoid the midday glare where possible. The mellow late afternoon sunshine is a great time to take pictures.
Where to buy film: Duty-free shops offer the best prices. Beware of out-of-date stock in local shops.

HEALTH

Insurance
Full medical insurance is highly recommended and should cover you for medical and hospital costs, transportation to a suitable off-island medical facility if required, repatriation and permanent disability. Note that you will need additional coverage for certain sports, such as scuba-diving.

Dental Services
Your medical insurance should cover emergency dental treatment, but it is worth having a check-up before you go. Ask the hotel or tourist office for a list of local dentists.

Sun Advice
A high-factor sun screen is a must for beachgoers, boat trips and just wandering around town. Go local and wear a straw hat and ensure that everyone (especially children) drinks plenty of water or soft drinks to combat dehydration.

Drugs
Travellers on prescription medication should ensure they have an adequate supply and a doctor's certificate. Pharmacies carry familiar over-the-counter US brand-name drugs, but check date stamps before purchasing. Coral cuts are easily infected, so clean thoroughly with antiseptic. To avoid being bitten by mosquitoes, use lavish applications of an insect repellent containing Deet before rain-forest excursions and cover up after dark.

Safe Water
Tap water is drinkable on most islands, though it is wise to buy bottled water and avoid iced drinks in less developed areas. Check the seals on mineral water bottles before purchasing.

CONCESSIONS

Students/Youths Many sights in the Caribbean offer discounted admission for children, but few extend concessions to foreign students. A student card may secure a modest reduction, but admission to most attractions is rarely more than US$1–2.

Senior Citizens Again, there are few concessions for senior citizens.

CLOTHING SIZES

USA	UK	Europe	
36	36	46	
38	38	48	
40	40	50	
42	42	52	Suits
44	44	54	
46	46	56	
8	7	41	
8.5	7.5	42	
9.5	8.5	43	
10.5	9.5	44	Shoes
11.5	10.5	45	
12	11	46	
14.5	14.5	37	
15	15	38	
15.5	15.5	39/40	
16	16	41	Shirts
16.5	16.5	42	
17	17	43	
6	8	34	
8	10	36	
10	12	38	
12	14	40	Dresses
14	16	42	
16	18	44	
6	4.5	38	
6.5	5	38	
7	5.5	39	
7.5	6	39	Shoes
8	6.5	40	
8.5	7	41	

123

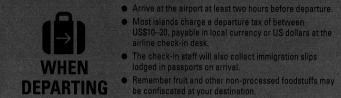

- Arrive at the airport at least two hours before departure.
- Most islands charge a departure tax of between US$10–20, payable in local currency or US dollars at the airline check-in desk.
- The check-in staff will also collect immigration slips lodged in passports on arrival.
- Remember fruit and other non-processed foodstuffs may be confiscated at your destination.

LANGUAGE

To say that English is the language of the former British colonies, Dutch is spoken in the Netherlands Antilles and that they speak French in the French Antilles is only half the story. Visit ex-British Dominica or St Lucia and the local patois sounds like French until you listen in. In fact it is Creole, a French-African hybrid with borrowed words and phrases from half-a-dozen other languages, and widely spoken in the Windward Islands and French Antilles. There are local variations from island to island, even village to village. English speakers will also find they fare no better trying to decipher Jamaican or Antiguan patois, despite its English roots.

However, English is the main language of the Caribbean tourist industry. It is spoken in most hotels in the French Antilles and the Spanish-speaking Dominican Republic and Puerto Rico, but little used outside the main tourist areas, where a phrase book would certainly come in handy. The bi-lingual Netherlands Antilles are equally at home in Dutch and English, but in Aruba, Bonaire and Curaçao, the islanders also speak Papiamento, a bizarre Creole language which continues to confound linguistic experts. The name Papiamento comes from the Spanish papia, meaning 'talk' or 'babble', and the language was developed as a sort of international pidgin by foreign merchants, missionaries and slaves combining elements of Spanish, Portuguese, French, Dutch, various Amerindian and African languages. Rather than Dutch, it is the mother-tongue of the three islands and taught in schools. Wherever you go in the Caribbean, you will find local people have time to stop and chat. There are jokey souvenir patois phrase books on sale, and most islanders appreciate – or at the very least are entertained – if you try out a few words.

Papiamento

bon bini	welcome	te aworo	see you later
bon dia	good morning	ayo	goodbye
bon tardi	good afternoon	masha danki	thank you very much
bon nochi	good evening	bunita	beautiful
con ta bai?	how are you?	hopi bon	very good
mi ta bon	I am fine	poco poco	quietly, slowly

Jamaican-style patois

Babylon	figures of authority like the police, or the established order (Church, State, Western culture)	limin'	hanging out, chatting with friends
		mash op	break, badly beaten, confused
bo-bo	foolish person	me wan fi go don ton	I want to go downtown to eat
boonoonoonoos	extraordinary, amazingly good	nyam	
chain (a)	not far (literally 22 yards)	one love	Rasta greeting
cho mon	no problem	riddim	rhythm
dreads	Rasta dreadlock hair	rass	backside (either very rude or affectionate)
duppy/jumby	ghosts and spirits	soon come	some time, take your time
herb/ganja	marijuana		
I an' I	we	tenky	thank you
irie	cool, peace, in harmony with the universe	walk good	parting expression
likkle	little	wine	dance with the hips in a sensual fashion

INDEX

Acknowledgements

The Automobile Association wishes to thank the following photographers and libraries for their assistance in the preparation of this book.

MARY EVANS PICTURE LIBRARY 10b; INTERNATIONAL PHOTOBANK 2, 6b, 15b, 23b, 27b, 32b, 35, 117b; MANNING SELVAGE AND LEE 21b (H P Merten); PICTURES COLOUR LIBRARY 7b, 8/9, 40, 52, 74, 76; REX FEATURES LTD 11b, 14b; SPECTRUM COLOUR LIBRARY 55b, 75b; LAWSON WOOD 17b; WORLD PICTURES LTD 20b, 36/7, 38, 39b, 49.

The remaining photographs are held in the Association's own photo library (AA PHOTO LIBRARY) and were taken by Peter Baker with the exception of the following: KIRK LEE ALDER front cover (a) dolphin; DAVID LYONS 8b, 12b, 12c, 22b, 26c, 30, 32a, 33, 34b, 50b, 51a, 69, 70a, 71b, 82/3, 87b, 91a, 92, 93, 94, 95, 96, 97, 98, 99, 100, 101, 102, 103, 104, 105, 106, 107, 108, 109, 110, 111, 112, 113, 114, 115, 116; LEE KAREN STOW front cover (c) windsurfer; ROY VICTOR front cover (g) woman, back cover boat, 9c, 13d, 42/3, 44b, 46b, 51c, 66b, 67b; JON WYAND Front cover (f) lily, bottom souvenirs, 5a, 6a, 6c, 7a, 8a, 9a, 10a, 12a, 13a, 13b, 13c, 14a, 16b, 27a, 28, 29, 31, 34a, 39a, 41, 42a, 42b, 43, 44a, 45, 46a, 50a, 51b, 66c.

Emma Stanford wishes to thank the tourist offices throughout the region for their invaluable help.

Page layout: Barfoot Design

Dear Essential Traveller

Your comments, opinions and recommendations are very important to us. So please help us to improve our travel guides by taking a few minutes to complete this simple questionnaire.

You do not need a stamp (unless posted outside the UK). If you do not want to cut this page from your guide, then photocopy it or write your answers on a plain sheet of paper.

Send to: **The Editor, AA World Travel Guides, FREEPOST SCE 4598, Basingstoke RG21 4GY.**

Your recommendations...

We always encourage readers' recommendations for restaurants, nightlife or shopping – if your recommendation is used in the next edition of the guide, we will send you a *FREE* AA *Essential* **Guide** of your choice. Please state below the establishment name, location and your reasons for recommending it.

_____

_____

_____

_____

Please send me **AA *Essential*** _____

(*see list of titles inside the front cover*)

About this guide...

Which title did you buy?

AA *Essential* _____

Where did you buy it? _____

When? m̲m̲ / y̲ y̲

Why did you choose an AA *Essential* Guide? _____

_____

_____

_____

_____

Did this guide meet your expectations?

Exceeded ☐   Met all ☐   Met most ☐   Fell below ☐

Please give your reasons _____

_____

_____

_____

continued on next page...

Were there any aspects of this guide that you particularly liked? _____

_____

_____

_____

Is there anything we could have done better? _____

_____

_____

_____

_____

About you...

Name (*Mr/Mrs/Ms*) _____

    Address _____

    _____ Postcode _____

    Daytime tel nos _____

Which age group are you in?
    Under 25 ☐   25–34 ☐   35–44 ☐   45–54 ☐   55–64 ☐   65+ ☐

How many trips do you make a year?
    Less than one ☐   One ☐   Two ☐   Three or more ☐

Are you an AA member? Yes ☐   No ☐

About your trip...

When did you book? m m / y y   When did you travel? m m / y y

How long did you stay? _____

Was it for business or leisure? _____

Did you buy any other travel guides for your trip?

    If yes, which ones? _____

_____

Thank you for taking the time to complete this questionnaire. Please send
it to us as soon as possible, and remember, you do not need a stamp
(*unless posted outside the UK*).

Happy Holidays!